TEXTING THROUGH TIME

A TREK WITH BRIGHAM YOUNG

For Morgan

J♥ Prophet

Christy Monson

TEXTING THROUGH TIME

A TREK WITH
BRIGHAM YOUNG

CHRISTY MONSON

Bonneville Books
An Imprint of Cedar Fort, Inc.
Springville, Utah

ISBN 13: 978-1-59955-916-2

Published by Bonneville Books, an imprint of Cedar Fort, Inc., 2373 W. 700 S., Springville, UT 84663
Distributed by Cedar Fort, Inc., www.cedarfort.com

LIBRARY OF CONGRESS CATALOGING-IN-PUBLICATION DATA

Monson, Christy, 1942- , author.
  Texting through time / Christy Monson.
    p. cm.
  Summary: Forbidden to touch their dad's new experimental time-traveling phone, Micah and Alicia play with it anyway and are sent back in time to eleven-year-old Brigham Young's family farm.
  ISBN 978-1-59955-916-2
  1. Young, Brigham, 1801-1877--Fiction. 2. Time travel--Fiction. 3. Text messages (Telephone systems)--Fiction. I. Title.
  PS3613.O5383T49 2011
  813'.6--dc23

                        2011030940

Cover design by Brian Halley
Cover design © 2011 by Lyle Mortimer
Edited and typeset by Kelley Konzak

Printed in the United States of America

10 9 8 7 6 5 4 3 2 1

Printed on acid-free paper

To children of God everywhere.

ACKNOWLEDGMENTS

I am grateful to my husband and children for their unfailing love and support. Thanks to my critique group for helping me become a better writer: Margaret Hovley, Marion Jensen, Chris Miller, Kendra Fowler, Cory Webb, Jeanette Wright, and Ken Lee. Rosalie Ledezma's artwork is wonderful. I feel honored that she would illustrate my book.

MALFUNCTION

MICAH and Alicia sat on a big rock in the shade of the pine tree in front of their house. Micah listened to the breeze whisper through the branches.

"See my new CTR ring?" asked Alicia.

Micah rolled his eyes. Alicia and her jewelry! "Let's have some fun," he said, putting his hand on a bulge in his pocket.

"What kind of fun?" asked Alicia, straightening her new beaded necklace.

"How about traveling into the future?"

"The future?" asked Alicia. She turned to Micah with her hand on her hip. "Wait a minute. Are you talking about Dad's new experimental phone? You know he's still working the bugs out of it for the company."

Micah smiled and pulled the phone from his pocket. "We're going to the future."

Alicia ran her fingers through her long brown hair, shoving it back from her face. "What's the matter with your brain? He told us not to use it."

"Hey," said Micah, "I can handle it—no problem. "Maybe I'll work the bugs out of it for him."

"You could really mess things up," said Alicia. "Remember, you have to find out about Brigham Young before Sunday School."

"I'll do it later," said Micah. "I wish I hadn't asked Sister Wilson why Brigham Young is called 'The Lion of the Lord.' I didn't think she'd want *me* to find out the answer. I thought she'd just tell us in class." He turned on the phone. PAST, PRESENT, and FUTURE buttons appeared on the screen. He pressed FUTURE. The phone lit and crackled and then turned black.

"Something's already wrong," said Alicia.

"No it's not," said Micah. He pressed the FUTURE button again—twice. The screen flashed. Micah stroked his thumb across the phone, and the screen began to scroll—faster and faster until he couldn't read it. He swiped his thumb back the other way to stop it.

A cow appeared on the screen. "Woof, woof," it said. Another crackle. "Cog," the phone said.

"Working well so far," said Alicia.

A duck blipped onto the screen. "Oink, oink." Static. "Puck," it said.

Alicia giggled.

"This is baby stuff!" Micah swiped his thumb across the screen again.

A rocket ship roared after a princess on a white horse.

"And you're going to trust this?" asked Alicia.

"Okay, okay, there're still some problems," said

Micah, "but I can handle it." He pressed the FUTURE button one more time.

The word PAST flashed on the screen. BIOGRAPHY lit up below it.

Alicia leaned in close. "Type in Brigham Young and see what happens."

"But I want to go to the future," said Micah.

"But it's not going to the future. Just type and see what it does," said Alicia.

Micah typed. The phone sparked and buzzed in his hand. Micah dropped it on the grass.

"Here, let me hold it," said Alicia, reaching down to pick it up.

"Hey, this was my idea," he said, putting his hand on the screen to take it away from her.

The phone vibrated, and Micah felt himself fading into gray fog with Alicia at his side. He grabbed for her hand. "I don't know where we're going."

"Now you've done it," said Alicia.

"Maybe we *are* going to the future." Micah's heart thumped. The screen on the phone went dark. He slipped it into his pocket. "I c-can handle it."

A black breeze swirled into the grayness. Micah felt weightless, tumbling over and over. Alicia's hands shook as she clutched at his arm.

"I feel dizzy—like we're falling through space," said Alicia. "What if we can't get back home?"

"We'll be okay," said Micah, breathing deeply. "We'll be fine."

A breeze blew the fog away. Micah could see the treetops below him. The tumbling changed to flying.

"We're zooming above the earth," said Alicia.

Micah held Alicia's hand as they drifted toward the ground. It was as if they had parachutes on. They toppled onto the grass.

"Where are we?" asked Alicia.

"I—I don't know," said Micah. His clothes felt strange. He looked down, surprised to see that he was wearing faded overalls with a hole in the knee and a yellow shirt. He wiggled his shoulders. The overalls were heavy and baggy. He was used to his shorts and T-shirt. His feet were bare. He scrunched his toes, feeling funny without his Crocs. Alicia had on a long dress with a matching sunbonnet.

"Pioneer clothes." Alicia giggled. "They feel different. I hope I don't trip over this dress. I like wearing shorts better." Her hand clutched her throat. "My necklace is gone." She looked at her hand. "So is my ring. I want my CTR ring."

Why is she worried about her jewelry at a time like this? thought Micah.

Alicia kicked at her skirt. "My dress is getting dirty because it's touching the ground."

The phone buzzed in Micah's pocket. He pulled it out and the screen lit up.

JUNE 1, 1812. BACKWOODS OF NEW YORK STATE. BRIGHAM YOUNG'S ELEVENTH BIRTHDAY.

"Wow," said Alicia. "This is the past."

"Oh no," said Micah, feeling disappointed. "I wanted to go to the future. The past is boring. Nothing exciting ever happened there." He pressed the FUTURE button again.

MALFUNCTION, the screen flashed.

Micah swiped his thumb across the screen.

JUNE 1, 1812. BACKWOODS OF NEW YORK STATE. BRIGHAM YOUNG'S ELEVENTH BIRTHDAY, appeared again.

He pressed the FUTURE button once more, and the screen went black. "We're trapped!"

TRAPPED

THEY stood at the edge of the woods, looking at a small cabin.

"Maybe this will be fun," said Alicia. "I'm a pioneer living on a farm." She twirled around in her full dress. Micah could be a grump if he wanted, but she was going to have a good time.

The sun peeked over the green treetops. A field of young corn shoots swayed in the breeze, and a patch of wild strawberries snuggled itself near the log cabin. A barefoot boy about their age stepped out of the front door, stretched, and yawned. His sandy hair tousled around his face. He wore tattered overalls, ragged at the bottom.

"Breakfast is ready, Brigham!" called a voice from inside.

"That must be Brigham Young," said Micah. "We *are* stuck in the past."

What if we can't get back? thought Alicia. *I guess this isn't so much fun. Micah and his big ideas!*

Micah pressed the FUTURE button one last time. The screen remained black. "Trapped!"

Brigham looked toward the trees where Micah and Alicia stood. He waved.

"He's seen us," said Micah. "Now we have to meet him."

"Well," said Alicia, "as long as we're here, we might as well get to know him."

"Brigham looks different than his pictures," said Micah. "He's young and thin, but he has the same round face—only without a beard."

"Of course," giggled Alicia. "He's only a boy. I wonder if he'll be friendly."

"Should we tell him where we came from?" asked Micah, slipping the phone in his pocket.

"I want to tell the truth," said Alicia, rubbing her finger where she wore her CTR ring.

"It would be easier to say we're new neighbors that moved in down the road."

"But that's not honest," said Alicia. "Do you want to lie to a prophet?"

"We better not tell him he'll be the prophet some-day," said Micah. "He doesn't even know about the Church yet."

"No one does," said Alicia. "The Church won't be organized until 1830. That's—" she stopped, cocking her head and counting on her fingers, "eighteen years from now."

Micah dug his toe into the dirt. "This is weird, but maybe it will be cool."

They walked toward Brigham.

"Hi," said Alicia, twisting her fingers together.

She took a deep breath to make the knot in her stomach go away.

"Good morning," said Brigham.

"I'm Micah, and this is my sister, Alicia."

"Do you live around here?" asked Brigham.

"We—we're from the future," said Micah, "and we just wanted to meet you."

"From the future? I don't understand."

"I don't understand either," said Micah. "It's hard to explain. I—I don't really know how it works."

"How did you get here?" asked Brigham.

"We have this phone," Alicia began.

Micah elbowed her. "Telephones aren't invented yet," he whispered.

"We have this electronic . . ."

"No electricity," murmured Micah.

Alicia put her hand on her hip. "Well, you try then." Maybe Micah could do a better job of explaining.

"We have this magic tablet," said Micah.

Alicia rolled her eyes.

"Magic tablet?" asked Brigham. "I don't know anything about magic."

"It's not a magic tablet," said Alicia, glaring at Micah. "Since we're from the future, we have things that you don't know about yet. Like glass bulbs that have lights inside so you don't need to use candles anymore and a box called a telephone that can carry your voice to people far away—even around the world. We also have a talking picture on a screen that can show men speaking from far away. Like for general conference when the prophe—"

Micah stepped on her foot.

"Rats!" Alicia covered her mouth with her hands. *I forgot for a minute that Brigham doesn't even know about the Church yet,* she thought.

"Rats?" asked Brigham, looking around. "I don't see any rats."

"She didn't really mean rats," said Micah. He crossed his eyes at Alicia.

"No rats," Alicia giggled. *I have to watch my mouth,* she thought.

Brigham smiled at Alicia. "There are rats in the barn." He scratched his head and turned to Micah. "Your being here does sound kind of like magic."

"Anyway," said Micah, "we have one of the things that will carry your voice to people a long ways away, and it has a FUTURE button. We pushed it and went to the past instead of the future. I guess it still needs some work."

Brigham looked puzzled.

Alicia threw her hands in the air. "We're pretty lame at explaining it to you."

"Lame?" asked Brigham. "You aren't lame. It looks like you can both walk."

We're getting nowhere with this conversation, thought Alicia. She sighed. "Maybe magic is the best answer."

"Things seem like magic when we don't know how they work," said Micah.

"Can we just be your friend and see what your life is like?" asked Alicia.

"I still don't understand how you got here," said Brigham. "Maybe it is magic. But it's nice to have some friends."

Micah looked down at his bare feet and then at

Brigham's bare feet. "Don't you wear shoes here?"

"I have a pair for Sunday," said Brigham, "but the rest of the week I go barefoot." He reached down and picked several strawberries growing in the garden and handed a few to Alicia and Micah.

"What do you do all day?" asked Micah.

"My brothers and I help my father clear the land for farming, and then we plant the crops," said Brigham. "It's a lot of hard work."

You won't always be a farm boy, Alicia wanted to say. Her mouth watered as she ate the sweet berries.

"Do you go to church?" asked Alicia.

"Oh, yes," said Brigham. "And I try to do what God wants me to do. My mother says 'God sends guardian angels to watch over us.'¹ So God takes care of me."

"Heavenly Father takes care of us too," said Alicia.

Brigham turned and walked toward the house. "Today is my birthday. I'm eleven, but no one has even wished me happy birthday. Maybe they forgot."

"Oh," said Alicia. "Happy birthday! Are you having a party?"

"No time for a party," said Brigham. "We have a large family, so we work all day long just to get enough food to eat. Besides, we aren't allowed to dance or even listen to violin music."²

Wow! thought Alicia. *I love to dance to music.*

"Breakfast, Brigham!" called the voice from the house again. "Who are you talking to?"

"Coming!" said Brigham. "Would you like to meet some of the family?"

"Sure," said Alicia.

They followed Brigham into the log cabin. A tall,

slender young woman with brown hair knotted at the back of her head turned from the stove. Her long gray skirt swished as she moved toward them. She smiled.

"Fanny, this is Alicia and Micah," said Brigham. "Fanny is my older sister."

A little girl hid behind Fanny's skirt. "This is Louisa. She's eight."

Louisa peeked out and smiled.

A small boy ran through the door carrying a worm. "I'll get you, Louisa," he yelled.

Louisa screamed and ran around Fanny and out the door.

"That's Lorenzo," said Brigham, laughing. "He's five."

"Greetings," said Fanny. "All we have for breakfast is a little mush, but you're welcome to some." She turned back to the stove, humming.

Alicia looked at the small bowls of plain oatmeal and thought of her sugar cereal and frozen waffles. "We've eaten," she said. *At home, I can eat all I want for breakfast,* she thought. *They must be poor. I never thought a prophet of God would be poor.*

Fanny handed Brigham a bowl. "Here's some mush. Hurry and eat so we can milk."

"Do I have to eat it now?" asked Brigham. "I want a little cream on it."

"You know there won't be any until after we milk," said Fanny. "And we need to save it to make butter."

Brigham sighed. "Dish up Mother's bowl."

Fanny handed him a bowl for his mother. "I'm going to the barn to get the milking started."

"I'll come as soon as I get Mother settled and

clean up the dishes," Brigham said.

Alicia watched Fanny walk out the door.

Brigham drizzled maple syrup over the cereal in his mother's bowl.

"I'd like you to meet my angel mother," said Brigham. "Let me see if she's ready to come to the table." He walked around a brown curtain strung across one end of the cabin.

"His mother's bed must be back there," whispered Alicia to Micah.

In a minute, Brigham parted the curtain with his elbow and came out, helping a frail-looking woman. She hobbled slowly, leaning on his arm. A smile brightened her pale face. Small brown curls peeked out from under her white, lacy bed cap.

Brigham guided her gently to a chair near the table, where she sat. She smoothed a wrinkle from her white nightgown.

"Mother, this is Alicia and Micah."

"Welcome," said Mrs. Young.

"Here's some oatmeal, Mother." Brigham pushed the cereal close to her and handed her a spoon. He plumped a pillow behind her back.

"You are so helpful," his mother said. "A blessing from Heavenly Father."

She coughed, spitting blood into her handkerchief.

My mother's never coughed up blood, thought Alicia, her stomach lurching. *I wonder if Brigham's mom is going to die.*

"I wish you felt better." Brigham turned his head away from his mother with a worried look on his face. "I don't want you to be sick." He took a deep breath and kissed her cheek.

Brigham really loves his mother, thought Alicia. *I need to remember to tell Mom how much I love her. I have a lot of blessings, and I don't even know it.*

"Fanny's already milking," said Brigham. "I need to go help her as soon as I clean up. And Father wants me to plant potatoes today."

"Looks like you children are here in time for the work, if you want to stay," said Brigham's mother.

As if we had a choice to leave, thought Alicia, glancing at Micah's worried face.

Micah frowned at her.

Brigham's mother went on. "When Brigham was a baby, he loved Fanny to take care of him. The cow also loved Fanny and would only let her do the milking. So Fanny used to hold Briggie on her hip and milk the cow with one hand."[3] His mother coughed—more blood.

After a couple of bites of cereal, she seemed tired and rested her head against the pillow at her back. Brigham brushed her wispy hair away from her face, tucking it inside her lacy cap.

"Thank you, son," she said.

"Let me get you to the rocking chair near the fire," said Brigham, helping her up. She settled into the rocker and closed her eyes.

Brigham began to put the breakfast dishes into a wash tub.

"I want to help," said Alicia.

"You can get a bucket of water from the pump outside to pour over the dishes if you want," Brigham said.

"I've never used one before," said Alicia.

"Just pump the handle and water will come out the spout."

Alicia ran outside and grabbed a wooden bucket sitting under the water pump. She pushed and pulled the handle up and down until water gushed out of the spout, spilling into the bucket. Alicia laughed. Getting water was fun.

When the bucket was half full, she carried it inside the house. "Do we need to heat the water to wash the dishes?"

Brigham swung a warming kettle out from the smoldering fireplace and poured the water into it. Steam hissed out into the room. When the water was hot, he splashed it over the dishes in the tub. He saved some in a bowl to the side for rinse water.

"I'll wash and you can dry," Brigham said, smiling at Alicia. "Are you sure you don't have to get home to do your own chores?"

I wish, thought Alicia.

Micah just stood there with his shoulders slumped, watching.

Alicia knew he was worried. "Don't you want to help too?" asked Alicia.

"Uh, sure," said Micah.

"You can sweep the floor," said Brigham. "The broom is over in the corner."

Micah got the broom.

"Thanks," said Brigham. "I'm glad you're here."

Our help will be his birthday

present, thought Alicia. "Will you teach me to milk?" asked Alicia.

"Milking?" asked Micah. Alicia could see him shake his head. He didn't want to milk.

3

TEXTING
JOURNAL

AS they walked to the barn, Micah lagged behind, pulling the phone from his pocket. *I don't want to do all this work*, he thought. *And besides, we've got to get out of here.* He stroked his thumb across the FUTURE button. FUTURE EVENTS appeared on the screen and below it a list:

MILKING COWS
PLANTING POTATOES
EATING SUPPER

He didn't want to milk or plant potatoes, so he clicked on SUPPER. Eating always sounded good, and maybe they could leave after they ate. The screen crackled. Fog crept in around him and blackness swirled, drawing Alicia back toward him. Brigham walked on ahead.

"What's going on?" shrieked Alicia. The blackness seemed to pull her to Micah's side. "I want to milk."

Brigham continued to the barn as if he hadn't heard Alicia or seen her leave.

Micah grabbed Alicia's hand, and they tumbled into the dark fog. As quickly as it had come, the fog blew away. Micah found himself seated on a gnarled oak log behind the Young cabin next to Alicia.

The sun dipped into the treetops.

"It's evening now," said Alicia, standing and brushing her skirt. "What happened?"

"I decided to get out of the work," said Micah.

"But that cuts me out too!" said Alicia. "I wanted to learn to milk."

Guilt crept from Micah's stomach up into his throat. He tried to swallow but couldn't.

Brigham trudged toward them. Dusty brown trails of dirt and sweat streaked his face. He looked tired. "Where did you go this morning?" He wiped his forehead. "On my way to the barn, I looked around, and you were gone."

"Uh—we left for a little while," said Micah, twisting his toe in the dirt and feeling uncomfortable.

Brigham stretched his back. "After milking, I plowed the entire south field and planted the potatoes."

We should have helped, thought Micah.

Alicia kicked Micah in the shin and glared at him.

That was a why-didn't-you-let-us-work-with-him look, thought Micah.

"Sounds like a hard day," said Micah, feeling rotten. He wanted to work hard, but he was in the habit of getting out of it whenever he could. He would try to do better—the very next time he had a chance.

Micah took a deep breath and changed the subject. "Do you go to school, Brigham?"

"I wish I could," said Brigham. "But I have to help with the farm."

"Oh," said Alicia. "I love going to school."

What would it be like to work all day instead of going to school? Micah shuddered at the thought.

"My mother taught me to read from the Bible, though." Brigham combed his hand through his sandy hair as they walked toward the house. "And now I love to read when I have time." Brigham washed the dirt from his hands and face at the water pump before they went inside.

"Come meet the rest of my family," said Brigham. "The day is almost done—the birthday no one in my family remembered. I guess everyone is too busy." Brigham sighed.

As they walked in the door, Brigham's sisters scurried in front of the kitchen cabinet like they were hiding something. Micah heard a dish clink onto a lower shelf and the cupboard shut.

"What are you hiding?" asked Brigham.

Fanny ignored his question and introduced Alicia and Micah to the rest of the family. "These are Brigham's sisters, Nancy, Rhoda, Nabby, and Susanna."

Louisa hid behind Susanna this time.

"John, Joseph, and Phineas work on other farms," said Fanny. "They'll be home soon. And this is Father Young." Fanny waved her arm toward a man sitting next to Brigham's mother.

Lorenzo skipped in carrying a grasshopper. Louisa squealed and ran.

"Hello," everyone said.

"I'm here," said Phineas. He walked in the door, holding a string of fish. "I've got dinner."

Everyone clapped.

Fanny smiled. "We went shopping." She waved the box in front of Brigham and then whisked it away as if teasing him. "Come visit with Mother and Father."

Brigham frowned and whispered to Alicia and Micah, "Why are my sisters buying themselves a new hat on my birthday?" He walked to his mother's rocker near the fireplace.

Micah and Alicia followed. Micah could smell bread baking in the oven.

Fanny smiled and turned to Brigham. "We churned your butter and made your bread while you were out in the potato field." She swung a kettle of water and potatoes over the fireplace to cook. "Thanks for cleaning the fish, Phineas."

Hot oil popped and spit at her as Nancy put the fish on to fry.

"Come tell me about your day while the girls finish cooking," said his mother.

Brigham's frown turned into a smile as he told his mother and father about planting the potatoes.

"Good work, son," said his father.

Micah felt guilty again. He could have made the day better for Brigham by helping.

"Dinner," called Fanny.

As Brigham turned to help his mother to the table, everyone began to shout.

"Happy birthday! Happy birthday!"

Brigham's face broke into a wide grin.

"He's happy now," whispered Alicia to Micah.

Fanny gave him the new hat box. "For you." She smiled and winked at him.

Brigham opened it. "A store-bought straw hat," he said. "My first ever!"

"It's your special day," said Fanny as Brigham sat at the table. She slid a pan from the lower cupboard shelves and placed it in front of him. "Your favorite, molasses cake."

Molasses cake? thought Micah. *Yuck!*

"Micah and Alicia, sit next to Brigham. You're the birthday guests," said Fanny.

"Everyone remembered your birthday," said Alicia.

Brigham smiled. "I shouldn't feel sorry for myself. I should have known they would remember."

The Young family, along with Alicia and Micah, had dinner.

Micah watched Alicia dig into her potatoes. He carefully pulled his piece of fish apart, taking out the tiny bones. He took a little bite and then another—no bones. *Good work*, he told himself.

Fanny set a section of the molasses cake in front of Micah. He made a face and looked around. Everyone seemed to be enjoying it. He didn't want to eat it, but he had to be polite. He took a small nibble. Sweetness filled his mouth. It was okay. He ate a bigger bite. It tasted a little bit like brown sugar. It wasn't as good as chocolate, but he liked it.

Father Young read a chapter from the Bible, and they sang together.

As it got dark, Micah said, "We'd better be going. Thanks, Brigham, for letting us meet your family today."[1] They walked out into the darkness.

"Where are you going?" asked Brigham. "My mother wants to know you are safe."

"Tell her we're going home," said Micah, "to find our parents—and I hope we are."

"With your magic tablet?" asked Brigham. "I still don't understand, but come back if you can. Thanks for celebrating my birthday."

Micah and Alicia waved to the family as they hiked toward the woods.

"They don't have parties like we do," said Alicia. "No balloons, no ice cream, and only one present."

"They're poor, but they seem happy," said Micah.

"I never thought that a boy who is going to become a prophet of God would feel sorry for himself—like I do sometimes," said Alicia.

"He really loves his mother," said Micah, "and he has plenty to do without an iPod."

They sat on a fallen log, and Micah took the phone from his overalls pocket.

"What do we do now?" asked Alicia.

"I don't know," said Micah.

"I thought you were going to troubleshoot the problems and work the bugs out."

"Okay, okay," said Micah, feeling guilty again. "I know we're in a mess, but maybe I can fix it." He clicked the phone on and pushed the FUTURE button again.

Crackle. The screen lit up. The words TEXTING JOURNAL REQUIRED flashed on the screen.

"What's a texting journal?" asked Alicia.

"I don't know," said Micah. He clicked on it to see what would happen.

TEXT THE THINGS YOU HAVE LEARNED TO YOUR PHONE AND LIST YOUR GOALS.

"I left my phone at home in the bathroom charging because the battery was dead," said Alicia. "Where's your phone?"

"Plugged in next to yours," said Micah. "I don't know how we can text to our phones. There are no cell towers around here."

"This whole thing is too weird," said Alicia. "We don't know how any of it works.

"Let's skip this part," said Micah. "I haven't learned anything but how to feel guilty for messing up. And I don't have any goals." He pressed the FUTURE button again.

TEXTING JOURNAL REQUIRED flashed again.

"No way," said Micah. "I'll bet Dad put this block on it. This is his way of making us learn life's lessons. Do you think he knew we'd take the phone?"

"I don't know," said Alicia, "but we have to do it." She took the phone in her hands and typed with her thumbs:

BRIGHAM'S BIRTHDAY PARTY, NO BALLOONS, ONE PRESENT.

THANKS FOR FOOD, BIRTHDAY PARTIES, MOM, WATER PUMP, HELP ME NOT FEEL SORRY FOR MYSELF.

She looked up at the screen, and it read

BRGHMS BDAY PRTY, NO BALLOONS, 1 PRESENT.

THX 4 FOOD, BDAY PRTYS, MOM, WTR PUMP. HLP ME NOT FEEL SRY 4 SELF.

"Micah, the phone changed my message to the old texting we used to do before we had a full keyboard to type on."

"No," said Micah, looking at the phone. "What else can go wrong?"

"This will be fun," said Alicia. "We haven't used the old texting for a long time." She clicked on her phone number and pushed SEND.

"So do I have to do it?" asked Micah.

He watched Alicia roll her eyes.

Micah sighed. "Fine." He typed:

BRIGHAM'S BIRTHDAY PARTY, BONY FISH, MOLASSES CAKE. I HATE TO WORK HARD. I LOVE YOU MOM. THANKS FOR HOME. I FEEL GUILTY FOR BEING HERE.

He looked at the screen.

BRGHMS BDAY PRTY, BONY FISH, MOLASSES CAKE. HATE 2 WRK HARD. <3 U MOM. THX 4 HME. GUILT 4 BEING HERE.

"It did the same thing for me," said Micah.

"At least we can read it," said Alicia.

Micah sighed. He hoped nothing else would go wrong. He clicked on his phone number and pushed SEND.

Fog rolled in and blackness swirled around them.

"Take us home," laughed Micah, talking to the phone. They tumbled into space.

HUNGRY
AND LONELY

A DENSE fog faded into blackness and covered them. A light breeze blew the haze away to reveal a bright sunny morning. Micah crashed through bare tree branches, landing in a grove of maples, the chill of winter still in the air. He rolled over in an icy patch of snow, watery from the spring thaw. His backside hurt from the hard fall. He stood up and stepped into a squishy mud puddle, his bare feet tingling with cold. "Brrr," he said, brushing the melting snow from his toes.

Alicia groaned beside him.

"This isn't home," said Micah, cracking a brittle branch with his foot.

"No kidding," said Alicia

Micah flicked a few slimy dead leaves off his feet. "I told the phone to take us home."

"It obviously wasn't listening," said Alicia.

Micah pulled the phone from his pocket. He typed in LOCATION. The phone lit and crackled.

BACKWOODS, SUGAR HILL, NEW YORK STATE, ABOUT 1815. EXACT DATE UNKNOWN.

"Not New York again," sighed Micah. Worry clutched at his stomach. "Why can't we get home?"

"I hope this isn't permanently our future," said Alicia. "I'm scared. Look at the mess you've got us into."

Guilt settled in the pit of Micah's stomach. He was sorry he'd taken the phone. *Change the subject*, he thought. "I wonder if Brigham is around here."

"At least he'd be a familiar face," said Alicia. "Besides, I want to know what happened to his mother. I wonder if she got better."

Footsteps rustled through the trees behind them. "I wish she would have," said a voice.

Micah turned. "Brigham!" He felt relief. But now he looked up at Brigham. At the birthday party, he and Brigham had been the same size. Today Brigham stood a head taller than Micah. His voice was deeper also.

"Hi, Brigham," said Alicia. "We're back, and I'm very glad to see you."

"How on earth did you get here?" asked Brigham.

"The magic tablet," said Micah.

"I still don't understand, but it's nice to see you." Brigham pointed to a boy behind him. "Remember Lorenzo? He's helping me today."

"Hello," said Lorenzo, his thin body towering above Micah.

"Got any worms or grasshoppers?" asked Alicia.

Lorenzo laughed.

"You both seem the same age you were when I

saw you last," said Brigham. "But that was several years ago."

"Like I told you before," said Micah. "We're from the future, and I don't know how this works."

"How you got here is very confusing," said Brigham.

Micah shook his head and frowned. "You think it's confusing to you. It's really confusing to us."

Brigham glanced at Lorenzo's questioning look. "I'll explain it to you later."

"How is your mother?" asked Alicia.

"She died about a year ago," said Brigham. His voice cracked, and he looked away.

"Life will never be the same again," said Lorenzo. "Father is gone much of the time now that he's moved us here to Sugar Hill."

Alicia traipsed around a tree, catching her dress on a broken branch and ripping a small hole in the tiny yellow flowers. "I'll bet you're lonely."

Brigham sighed and didn't answer for a moment. "It's spring, and the sap is running in the sugar maples. We have a lot of trees to tap so we can boil the sap into syrup and sugar. Do you want to help?"

"Sure," said Alicia.

Micah dug his toe into the decaying leaves and mud. Here was a chance for him to work so he wouldn't feel guilty again. Why was it so easy for Alicia to jump in to help? He would never understand that.

Brigham picked up his drill. "I'm going to bore a hole in each of these trees and put a spout with a bucket on the end to catch the sap draining from the tree."

"Is that how you get maple syrup?" asked Alicia.

"I've always wondered how it came out of the trees."

"It's not maple syrup until we boil it down," said Lorenzo. "It takes forty buckets of sap to cook down to one bucket of syrup."

"Wow," said Alicia. "That's a lot of boiling."

Lorenzo smiled. "I'm going to start a fire under the kettle."

"While Lorenzo gets the fire going, we'll drill the holes in the trees and hang the buckets," said Brigham."

"Great," said Alicia. "This will be fun."

"Let's start at the north end of the grove and work toward the south," said Brigham, beginning to drill into the trees. "Here, Micah, you pound the plugs in, and Alicia, you can put the buckets on."

What have I gotten myself into? thought Micah. After a few trees, his arms began to feel stiff from pounding. *Work stinks!*

The sun struggled higher, melting more snow. A small stream meandered through one side of the grove down toward the cabin.

As soon as the buckets were full, Brigham carried them back to Lorenzo's big kettle of boiling syrup and dumped them in.

"Let me carry one," said Alicia. "It will save you a trip."

"Thanks," said Brigham.

I guess I'd better offer to carry some too, thought Micah. *I don't want Alicia to show me up.* Micah lifted a heavy bucket of sap and sloshed it to the fire, where Lorenzo dumped it into the boiling cauldron.

"That looks like a witch's brew," said Alicia.

"Don't talk about witches," said Brigham, shivering. "That's scary. They used to burn witches at the stake."

"Sorry," said Alicia.

After a while, the four of them rested in the shade of a tree near the cabin and drank icy creek water from a tin cup Brigham had tied to his waist. The water chilled the metal cup in Micah's hands. He gulped two mugs to quench his thirst. Then he let the third one drizzle over his tongue and down his throat. *Cool!* he thought, *In more ways than one.* He laughed at his own joke.

"I don't know if you want to help us all day," said Brigham. "Lorenzo and I have no lunch, and there's no food at home. Everyone is gone. The girls are with

Rhoda and her husband, and the boys are working on other farms. Father has taken sixty pound of sugar to town to sell."

"We'd like to stay and help you," said Alicia.

"You'll get hungry," said Brigham.

"That's okay," said Alicia.

Micah didn't want to work hard and be hungry. Why did he promise himself he'd start to work now? This was a rotten time to learn to help. Maybe he should push the future button to another time. *No,* he told himself. *I need to learn to work. But I don't have to like it like Alicia does.*

"Thanks, Alicia," said Brigham. He put his hand on Micah's shoulder. "Thanks, Micah."

"You're welcome," said Micah. Well, maybe it was okay to help a future prophet of God.

Micah and Alicia helped Brigham carry bucket after bucket to the fire, where Lorenzo stirred the syrup. Micah's shoulders ached, and the muscles in his arms burned from lifting the heavy buckets.

"The sun's setting," said Brigham. "We'll call it a day. The kettle is full, and it'll have to boil down before we add more."

Micah and the others plodded toward the cabin. Hunger pangs cramped Micah's stomach until he could hardly breathe. *Maybe we'll starve to death if we don't get the phone working,* he thought.

As they neared the cabin, Brigham pointed to a small robin in a nearby tree. "Dinner," he whispered.

"What?" asked Micah. *There's nothing in that tree to eat,* he thought. He can't mean that little bird. How could four of them eat a robin for dinner? At home there was no way he would even think of eating a song bird, but he'd never been as hungry as he was right now—ever in his life. It would be a small meal, but it would be better than nothing.

"Stay here," murmured Brigham, edging toward the cabin door. "I have to get my father's old muzzle-loader. I'll be right back."

Brigham slipped into the house and returned with the gun. Taking careful aim, Brigham squeezed the trigger. *Boom!* The robin fell.

"I can't believe you killed a robin to eat," said Alicia.

"It's dinner," said Brigham.

They tramped to the cabin, where Brigham plucked and cleaned the bird and boiled it in some water.

"Dump the empty flour barrel over the pot, Lorenzo," said Brigham. "I think there's a little flour dust to make a stew."[1]

Brigham poured each of them a bowl. As Micah spooned the soup into his mouth, he thought of the fridge full of food at home. He could snatch a cheese stick or an apple whenever he wanted. He had never felt this thankful for food before—even on fast Sunday. But from now on he would.

The watery bird broth eased Micah's hunger pangs, but not by much. "Thanks for dinner. We're going to try again to get home."

"Do you want to use your magic tablet here in the house so I can see it?" asked Brigham.

Micah twisted his fingers. "It's better if we're alone in the woods because I don't know if the pho—uh, magic tablet will work right."

"Well, I hope you make it," said Brigham.

"See you," said Alicia.

They walked into the dark evening.

"Brigham is hungry and lonely," said Alicia, "and so am I. I'm glad we have enough food to eat and a family that stays home—if we ever get back there."

Micah traipsed toward the woods again and sat on a fallen log with Alicia. He pushed the FUTURE button. *Crackle.* The screen lit up. TEXTING JOURNAL REQUIRED flashed on the screen.

Micah began to text:

GATHERD MAPL SAP. ATE ROBIN SOUP. WRKD HARD, MISS HME.

HNGRY, HNGRY, HNGRY.

It didn't matter if he typed the entire word out, the phone made the texting abbreviation. He hit send.

Alicia's turn:

BRGHMS MOM DIED. WRKD HARD. ATE A BIRD.

XOXO MOM, ARMS TIRD, HNGRY, THX 4 BIRDS, HRD DAY—

NO SRY 4 SELF.

She sent it. "What do we do now?" asked Alicia.

"If I press the FUTURE button again, I don't know where we'll go," said Micah. "It hasn't taken us home so far, so who knows where we'll end up? But when I stroked the FUTURE button outside the barn instead of pressing it, I got a list of future events."

"At least we'd have a choice," said Alicia.

Micah swiped the button. Alicia leaned in so she could see the screen. FUTURE EVENTS appeared. Below it was a list:

BRIGHAM YOUNG LEFT HOME AGE 16, WORKED AS
A CARPENTER

BRIGHAM MARRIED MIRIAM WORKS, TWO
DAUGHTERS

MIRIAM GOT CONSUMPTION, BRIGHAM CARED FOR
HER

"Hey, look, Brigham's wife got sick just like his
mother, and he took care of her," said Alicia.

BRIGHAM LOOKED FOR A CHURCH LIKE CHRIST
ORGANIZED

SAMUEL SMITH FIRST MISSIONARY FOR THE CHURCH
GAVE BRIGHAM'S BROTHER PHINEAS A BOOK OF
MORMON

BRIGHAM READ THE BOOK OF MORMON, KNEW IT
WAS TRUE

BRIGHAM BAPTIZED APRIL 14, 1832

MIRIAM BAPTIZED, THEN DIED.

"That's sad," said Alicia.

BRIGHAM AND HIS FRIEND HEBER C. KIMBALL MEET
JOSEPH SMITH

"Press that one," said Alicia. "I want to see the
Prophet Joseph Smith."

"Me too," said Micah. He pressed the button, and
fog rolled in, swirling blackness around them. They
plummeted into space.

5

MEETING JOSEPH SMITH

ALICIA and Micah tumbled onto the front lawn of a white house with a picket fence.

KIRTLAND, OHIO. 1833, the phone flashed. Micah put it in his pocket.

Alicia looked down at her clothes, expecting to see faded yellow flowers on her dress again. Instead she had on a plain blue dress with long sleeves. It had buttons up the front and a little white lace collar. She felt her neck and fingers—still no necklace or CTR ring. She wished for home.

Micah wore brown pants and a cream-colored shirt. He patted his stomach. "It's funny, I don't feel hungry anymore—not like I did when we were with Brigham."

"I'm not hungry either," said Alicia, "and I'm glad we can decide where to go now."

"If we could only figure out how to get back home," said Micah.

"I'm beginning to think I'll never see Mom again,"

said Alicia. "Even if we can jump a few years ahead for each scene, it's going to take forever to get to our time."

"When I'm in trouble, you always say, 'make the best of it,'" Micah said, imitating her.

"I hate those words right now," said Alicia. "Why did this have to happen to us?" They were trapped, like Micah said. She rubbed her finger where she usually wore her CTR ring. Here she was, feeling sorry for herself again. Would she ever stop? Maybe she should try to make the best of it.

She looked at the small white frame house in front of her. There were woods all around—not thick, dark woods, but trees scattered on the hillside accented with green undergrowth.

A wagon jolted up the road and stopped in front of the house. The man driving looked like Brigham Young.

"Here we are, Heber," the man said. "This is the house."

It was Brigham's voice. "Brigham," said Alicia and Micah together. They ran to him. *Brigham looks more and more like the pictures I've seen of him*, thought Alicia. *I wonder if he'll remember us.*

"Alicia and Micah," said Brigham. He seemed surprised to see them as he jumped down out of the wagon and bent down to hug them. "You're still young, just like you were on my eleventh birthday."

He remembered, thought Alicia.

"We know," sighed Micah.

"This is my friend, Heber Kimball," said Brigham. "Alicia and Micah are friends of mine from New York."

Heber reached out and shook their hands. "Nice to meet you children," he said.

"Heber, if you'll tie the horses, I'll see if Joseph Smith is home," said Brigham. He and Alicia and Micah walked up the path to the house.

"I see you still didn't make it home," said Brigham. "I'm worried about you being alone."

"We're okay," said Micah. "I just don't know what's wrong with the magic tablet."

"Well, you can always stay with me if you need to," said Brigham. "I'll help you any way I can."

"Thanks," said Micah.

"I have some exciting news," said Brigham. "I've found the true Church—with the same organization as in the time of Christ. I have found our Savior's Church."

"We know," said Micah. "Remember, we're from the future."

"So you love Jesus Christ just like I do." Brigham rubbed his forehead.

"We love Jesus," said Alicia, touching her finger where her CTR ring usually went.

"I'm glad you know about the Church," said Brigham.

"Yes," said Alicia. "We're members." *And you're going to be the prophet after Joseph Smith*, she thought, but she didn't say anything.

"Then you know about Joseph Smith," said Brigham. "This is his house. I'm looking forward to meeting him."

They walked together up the steps to the front door. Brigham knocked. Heber joined them.

A tall, slender woman answered. Her dark hair highlighted her smooth white skin. She held a little girl with curly blonde hair in her arms.

"May I help you?" the woman asked.

Emma, thought Alicia. *You're beautiful.*

"Yes," said Brigham. "We're looking for Joseph Smith."

The woman smiled. Her eyes were kind. "I'm his wife, Emma," she said.

"I'm Brigham Young, this is Heber Kimball, and these are my friends Alicia and Micah."

"Welcome to our home," said Emma. "Joseph's out in the woods chopping firewood."

"Thanks," said Brigham.

The four of them left the front steps and hurried into the woods.

Alicia had to run to keep up. "You're walking very fast, Brigham," she said.

Brigham laughed and slowed his steps. "I guess I am. I'm excited to meet the prophet." He took her hand and helped her over a fallen log.

"I'm excited too," said Alicia.

In the distance, they heard the sound of an ax chopping.[1] When the prophet came into view, they stopped.

"I don't know what I expected," said Brigham. "He seems like an ordinary man."

Alicia stood and looked at Joseph Smith. The sunlight streamed down on him. His broad shoulders and blond hair accented his tall, muscular body. Wood chips flew from his ax as it struck the log. He turned when he saw them. His wide smile greeted them.

"Hello," said the prophet.

A shiver went through Alicia.

"I'm Brigham Young, and this is Heber Kimball," said Brigham, hurrying forward. He reached out to shake Joseph's hand. "This is Alicia and Micah."

"How blue the prophet's eyes are," whispered Alicia to Micah.

Alicia's whole body tingled—like fast Sunday when she wanted to bear her testimony. The Prophet Joseph Smith stood next to her. The Holy Ghost was witnessing that Joseph Smith was a prophet of God.

She heard Brigham whisper to Heber, "I'll remember this meeting all my life."

Joseph put his hand on Brigham's shoulder. "I

know I've just met you, but the Spirit tells me you will be a leader in the kingdom of God someday."[2]

He will, Alicia wanted to say. *He'll be the prophet after you.*

The Prophet Joseph took Alicia's hand. "It's nice to meet you."

"Did you really see Heavenly Father and Jesus?" asked Alicia.

Joseph's eyes seemed to smile and look deep inside Alicia. "I really did." He turned to Micah. "It's nice to meet you, young man."

Micah grinned. "Thanks for translating the Book of Mormon. We read it every night before bed."

"It will give you a strong testimony," said Joseph. "When you read the scriptures, the Holy Ghost teaches you the truth of all things."

Alicia smiled. Tears of happiness almost spilled out of her eyes. Just like Brigham, she would never forget this moment.

Joseph put his arm around Micah and turned back to Brigham and Heber. "Let me show all of you the temple site. The foundation is finished, and the walls are about halfway up. The Kirtland Temple will be the first since the time of Christ."

They walked from the woods, and Brigham drove his wagon to the temple grounds.

The building stood—stately with stone blocks reaching out of the ground.

"First we made bricks to build the temple," said Joseph, "but they crumbled. Then we found this sandstone." He patted the rock. "As you can see, big blocks were cut for the walls. We are going to cover them with plaster."

TEXTING THROUGH TIME

"Looks very sturdy," said Brigham.

"And beautiful as well," said Joseph. "I'm going to ask all the young people to gather pottery and dishes. We'll crush them into a fine powder to mix with the plaster to make it sparkle. I see it being a blue-gray color."[3]

"How pretty," said Alicia.

"We must make it the very best," said Joseph.

"Since Christ had a temple, it stands to reason that there should be one today," said Brigham.

"The Son of Man had no place to lay his head," said the prophet. "And now He shall have one."

"We build houses for ourselves," said Brigham. "Now let's build one for our Lord and Savior."[4]

"Micah, I can feel the spirit of the temple," said Alicia.

"It's going to be a very special place," said Micah.

"Let's go back to the house," said the prophet. "I have so much to tell you about the Church."

"We'd love to stay a few days and learn more," said Brigham.

"We need to go now and get back to our family," said Micah. "Thanks for showing us the temple site." Micah nudged Alicia. "Let's get going. Maybe we can get home."

"It's nice to meet you," said Alicia to Joseph Smith. She was glad Micah didn't want to wait a few days. She missed home so much.

"It was wonderful to meet you," said Joseph. "I can tell both of you have a testimony of the gospel."

They waved good-bye and walked toward a nearby field.

"I know what I want to do after seeing the Prophet Joseph Smith," said Alicia. "I'm going to write my testimony in my journal."

"I'm going to go to the temple to do baptisms for the dead," said Micah.

"I wish I were old enough," said Alicia.

"Only one more year until you're twelve, and then you can."

"It seems like a long time to wait," said Alicia. "You always get to do things before me. I don't like waiting outside while you get to go in the temple." She stopped. "Oh, oh, there I go feeling sorry for myself again." She looked at Micah. "I'm glad there's a temple close for me to go to, if we ever get home—and I'm going the day I turn twelve."

"I'll go with you," said Micah.

They sat down in a field, and Micah pulled the phone out of his pocket. "Where to next?"

"Home," said Alicia.

"I don't think that's a choice," said Micah, swiping the FUTURE button.

TEXTING JOURNAL lit the screen.

Micah typed:

MET JOSEPH SMITH, KNOW HE IS A PROPHET.

THX 4 JS, THX 4 B OF M—READ EVRY DAY. THX FOR TMPLS.

He hit send.

Alicia typed:

MET EMMA SMITH & PROPHET JOSEPH. EMMA = BEAUTIFUL.

HLP ME NOT FEEL SRY 4 SELF AGAIN. TSTMNY—
THX 4 JS, BY, B OF M, TMPLS, AND THE SAVIOR.

She hit send.

Micah stroked the FUTURE button again. FUTURE
EVENTS appeared on the screen.

MISSION TO CANADA—TRAVELED 250 MILES IN
MUD AND SNOW

Alicia shivered. "Let's not go there."

MISSION TO EASTERN STATES

MISSION TO ENGLAND—SEASICK ON THE OCEAN

"Not seasick," said Micah.

THOUSANDS CONVERTED TO THE CHURCH IN
ENGLAND

"Look," said Alicia, "there's a QUOTE button flash-
ing. Press it and see what it says."

Micah pushed it. A voice began to speak. It was
Brigham's.

"I wanted to thunder and roar out the Gospel to
the nations. It burned in my bones like fire pent up, so
I [began] to preach. . . . Nothing would satisfy me but
to cry abroad in the world, what the Lord was doing
in the latter days."[3]

"That's Brigham's voice," said Alicia. "He loved
missionary work."

"How did the phone get a soundtrack of his voice?"
asked Micah.

"There were no recordings in his day," said Alicia.

"I guess the phone picked up his voice when we
were with him," said Micah.

"It's got a microphone, I'm sure," said Alicia.

"That's cool," said Micah. "The phone heard his voice and put it to one of his quotes."

"Wow," said Alicia. "This phone's not completely broken."

"So why can't it get us home?" asked Micah.

They looked back at the phone.

JOSEPH SMITH'S DEATH

"Not that," said Alicia. "That's too sad."

WINTER QUARTERS, NEBRASKA

TREK WEST APRIL 1847

"That one," said Alicia.

Micah pressed the button.

They tumbled into gray fog surrounded by blackness.

HIGH WATER

ALICIA felt herself falling out of the sky. A churning river boiled below her. Fear gripped her. Would she drown? She landed in the water with a splash, gulping air in shock and surprise. As she sank into the raging water, her dress clung to her neck and head, smothering her. Panic filled her. She thrashed her arms to move her dress off her face. Kicking her feet to thrust herself upward, she devoured the air when she reached the surface.

The bank rushed past as the water swept her downstream. Gasping and choking, she blinked the water out of her eyes and looked around. The river's swift current hurled her along.

Someone on the bank shouted, "Get that girl!"

A horse galloped downstream ahead of her and plunged in. As she rushed by, the rider reached out and grabbed her arm, slinging her behind him on the swimming horse. She clung to the saddle and scrambled up on the horse's rump.

"I've got her," he yelled.

The voice sounded familiar. "Brigham?" asked Alicia as she sat upright and clung to his waist, shaking.

Brigham turned and looked at her, fear on his face. "Alicia, you ended up in a very scary place."

Alicia clung to his waist to stop her shivering. She laid her head on his back, feeling safe but wishing it were her father.

The horse swam toward the shore. Alicia could feel the horse's hooves touch the bottom of the river-bed and the safety of the water's edge. She pushed the hair back from her face. "Where's Micah?"

"That I don't know," said Brigham, scanning the pioneer company.

"There he is," yelled Alicia. Micah waved to them from the riverbank as he dumped dirt from his shoes. *At least he has shoes this time*, she thought. *What if he'd landed in the water and gotten the phone wet? Then it wouldn't work at all and we'd be in big trouble.*

Brigham trotted his horse over by Micah. He swung Alicia down and dismounted.

Micah hugged Alicia. "Are you okay? I was so scared when I saw you land in the water."

"I'm still shaking," said Alicia, clinging to him and wanting to go home.

"Sit here by me and rest," said Micah, rubbing her back.

Alicia felt the warm sun as she sat, but she was still cold and continued to shiver.

Brigham put his jacket around her. "I guess you are going to follow me the rest of my life. Just land someplace safer next time."

"We are obviously not home," said Alicia.

"Where are we?" asked Micah.

"You landed smack in the middle of the Platte River," said Brigham. "We've followed the water all the way from Winter Quarters, and now we need to cross it to get to Fort Laramie."

"Thanks for the rescue," said Alicia. "I'm feeling a little better."

"You're welcome," said Brigham. "You two are having quite the adventure."

"I guess," said Micah.

Alicia could see wagons lined up behind them across the prairie. Men got down from their wagon seats and began to unhitch their teams.

Brigham touched Alicia's shoulder. "You two stay back here until we get organized. Then my wife will find you some dry clothes."

Brigham climbed on a nearby wagon tongue and called to the men. "Animals have to cross first."

Several of the men on horseback drove the horses, oxen, and cows forward from the wagons, bringing them together in a herd surrounded with a haze of dust.

Alicia coughed.

The animals moved toward the riverbank. But as soon as they reached the water, they circled back into the herd. A chorus of mooing and neighing filled the air. A man on horseback nosed his horse forward, nudging an ox toward the water. The ox hesitated.

"Yahhh," yelled the man, flicking the ox with his whip.

The ox bellowed and lunged into the water, and

the rest of the herd followed. Their heads bobbed above the water as they swam to the other side.

"The water is very high," said one man. "How'll we get the wagons across?"

"We may have trouble," said Brigham. "But let's try tying four wagons together. If we tie ropes to the wagon tongues, we can float them across."

"Micah," said Brigham, "Please ask my wife, Clara, to give you the ropes I have in the back of the wagon." Brigham pointed. "It's the one right over there."

Micah ran to get them.

"Alicia," said Brigham, "Will you ask Clara for the buffalo hides I've cut into strips? We'll lash the wheels together with them."

Alicia hurried over to the wagon.

Sister Young turned from handing the ropes to Micah. "Hello," she said.

"Hello, Sister Young. I'm Alicia."

Sister Young had a long, full face and a prominent nose. Her brown hair was tied at the back of her head in a bun. She seemed almost as tall as Brigham.

"Brigham—uh—Brother Young wants the buffalo hides he cut into strips," said Alicia.

"They're right here," said Clara with a smile. "I'd give you some dry clothes, but we don't have any. We only have two children in the entire company. The sun will have to dry you out."

"It's okay," said Alicia. "I'm almost dry—except my skirt."

Another woman walked up to the wagon. "This is another Sister Young, Lorenzo's wife, Harriet," said Clara.[1]

Even Lorenzo has grown up, thought Alicia.

"What are you two children doing way out here?" Harriet asked. "Are you from one of the wagon trains following the Oregon Trail?"

"Hello, Sister Young," said Alicia. "We're not going to Oregon, but we're a long way from home. How we got here is very confusing."

"Well, I hope you get out of this barren land soon. I really don't like it myself," Harriet said. "It's all sagebrush and desert."

I guess everyone isn't happy to be going west, thought Alicia. "I'd better get this buffalo hide to Brother Young."

"It was nice to meet you," said Harriet.

"We'll see you again," said Clara.

Alicia ran back to Brigham and handed him the lashing. The men had already emptied all the supplies out of the wagons and roped the tongues together. Several riders swam their horses across the river with the lead rope ahead of the wagons to guide them across. As soon as the wheels of the four wagons were bound together with the lashing, the men launched them into the river. They floated steadily at first, but in the deep current, they began to wobble. The men couldn't hold them straight.

"The current's tossing those wagons around like they're logs," said Brigham.

The wagons flipped end over end.

"Drag them back to shore before the water dashes them to pieces," yelled Brigham.

The men tied the ropes to a team of horses. In a tug-of-war between the horses and the river, the toppled wagons struggled back to shore. When they were on the bank, the men began to unhook them.

"Maybe we can build a raft to ferry the wagons across one at a time," said one man.

The sun moved across the sky as the men chopped down some small trees near the river and skinned the branches off.

Alicia followed Brigham while he undid the lashings from the toppled wagons.

"Hold these leather strips until the men are ready to tie the raft together," said Brigham.

Alicia gathered the leather strips and handed them to the men.

Micah steadied the logs while the men lashed them with the buffalo leather.

Alicia watched Micah. It looked like hard work to hold the logs together. She wondered if Micah liked doing it.

The men launched the raft with a wagon on it. In the middle of the river, the water ripped the logs apart and dropped the wagon into the swift current. The team of horses dragged the wagon back to the shore.

Brigham took his hat off and wiped his brow. "We'll need a stronger raft to ferry the wagons across." He pointed to the hills. "I saw a stand of white pine and cottonwood to the east. Let's go cut some big logs."

"Can we help?" asked Alicia.

"I'd love your help," said Brigham. He mounted his horse. "Alicia, climb up behind me, and Micah, get behind Brother Willard Richards. After we fell the trees, you two can skin off the branches with my hatchet and smooth the logs with a drawknife while we cut the next tree."

Clara walked toward Brigham's horse and handed him a flour sack. "Lunch," she said. "I don't want you to be hungry."

"Thanks," said Brigham, twisting the top of the sack and tying it to the saddle horn. "Work and hunger don't go together." He looked at Micah and winked.

"We know that," said Micah. "Do you remember carrying buckets of maple syrup and then having nothing to eat but the bird broth?"

"I remember," said Brigham. "Those were hard times."

Brigham took his foot from the stirrup so Alicia could swing herself up behind him. Alicia settled on the horse and looked down at the ground. "It's a little scary up here."

Brigham laughed. "Hold on," he said and nudged the horse forward.

Alicia looked over at Micah. He smiled as he climbed up on the back of Brother Richards's horse. They headed for the hills along with other men.

As the horses climbed, their breath came in short heavy bursts. White lather covered their back sides. *Carrying two people is hard work*, thought Alicia. Soon they reached a stand of tall pines.

"These are good trees," said Brigham. "Let's cut here."

Men dismounted. Brigham found a sturdy tree, looked at the way it leaned, and began to chop.

"Brother Brigham's notching a 'V' on the tilted side so it will fall that direction," said Brother Richards.

"You kids stand back until it's down, and then you can clear off the branches."

After much chopping, there was a loud *crack* and the tree fell.

"Here's a hatchet," said Brigham to Micah. "Chop off the branches."

"Where's my drawknife?" asked Alicia. "I don't even know what one looks like."

Brigham pulled a long metal blade from a leather pouch. It had handles on both ends perpendicular to the long knife. "Scrape this along the log to smooth out the knots and bumps where the branches were. Use both hands and draw the knife toward you." Brigham showed her how.

"I can do that," said Alicia.

The men cut tree after tree. Sweat dripped from under their hats and streaked down their backs. Micah hacked the branches off the main trunk, and Alicia smoothed each log with the drawknife. Wood shavings covered her dress, and she picked a few bark curls out of her hair.

They sat in the shade of the trees for lunch. Alicia turned her face into the cool breeze and shivered as her sweat dried. It felt good to work hard.

After the logs were all cut and cleaned, the men tied them together for the pack horses to drag to the river.

"Everyone is working hard," said Micah.

"Everyone has to work hard or we won't survive," said Brigham.

When they finished, Alicia climbed onto Brigham's horse, and the group started back. Micah and Brother Richards rode beside them.

"Why doesn't God make it easier for you to get across the river?" Micah asked Brigham. "He could make the water slow down if He wanted to, or He could guide the wagons across so they wouldn't flip over."

"Ah," said Brigham. "Wouldn't it be nice if God did our work for us? But He has done His share by giving us the trees to build a raft and the horses to haul them to the river.[2] Remember what happened to Nephi? He had to go back to Jerusalem three times to get the brass plates from Laban, and finally kill him. The Lord didn't just hand the plates over." Brigham turned in the saddle to look at Micah. "If we do the work to lead the Saints to Zion, we will be blessed."

"I want to work so I'll be blessed too," said Alicia.

"It takes all kinds of work to build Zion—mental, physical, and spiritual," said Brigham.

"How do you think I'll be blessed?" asked Alicia.

"Alicia, the real blessing of labor is what you become, not the work itself," said Brigham. "Toil makes us strong and confident so we feel good about ourselves."

"I'm beginning to like work," said Micah.

Brigham smiled.

"Only beginning," Micah mouthed to Alicia when Brigham had turned.

Back at the river's edge, Brigham and Brother

Richards lashed the logs together, notching cross pieces to make the large raft solid. It looked strong and sturdy. The men rolled a wagon onto it and slowly launched it into the swift river. Ropes steadied the ferry as it made its way into the deep part of the water. The raft lurched and twisted sideways. The men held the ropes taut.

Will it make it? wondered Alicia.

The craft kept going until it reached the other side.[3] A cheer went up from the pioneers. Brother Richards shook Brigham's hand and slapped his back. "We did it," he said, laughing.

"God blessed us," said Brigham. "Let us thank Him."

The sun dipped into the western sky as everyone knelt in prayer.

Brigham raised his voice to thank Heavenly Father for His help, and the prairie was still.

After the prayer, Alicia put her arms around Brigham and hugged him tight. "Thanks for letting us help—and thanks for saving me from the river."

"You're very welcome," said Brigham.

"Thanks," said Micah, shaking his hand. "I think we'll try to get home again."

"I wish you well," said Brigham. "Thanks for your help today. Maybe I'll see you again."

"I want to get home," said Alicia.

They walked to the back of the wagons and sat in the twilight.

Micah pulled out the phone and began to text:

BRGHM BUILT A STRNG RAFT TO CROSS RIVER.

GOD WANTS US 2 WRK HRD.

BEGN 2 LIKE WRK, FEEL GOOD INSID, THX 4 LOGS & HORSES.

Alicia's message:

BRIGHAM SAVED ME FROM THE RIVER. WAS SCRD.
<3 WRK, NO SRY 4 SELF. I <3 BRGHAM, MISS U HOME.

The screen lit. PAST, PRESENT, FUTURE.

"Don't even think about pressing PAST or PRESENT," said Alicia. "I don't want to go further back, and I don't want to stay here in the present."

"I wasn't going to press either of those," Micah said. He swiped the FUTURE button. FUTURE EVENTS appeared.

BRIGHAM SICK WITH COLORADO TICK FEVER

SAINTS PRAY FOR BRIGHAM TO GET WELL

BRIGHAM ENTERS THE VALLEY "THIS IS THE RIGHT PLACE"

BRIGHAM DEDICATES SALT LAKE TEMPLE SITE

SAINTS PLANT CROPS

INDIANS STEAL HORSES, BEG FOR FOOD

BRIGHAM FEEDS INDIANS, BLESSES THEM

"Let's check out the Indians," said Micah.

"Scary," said Alicia, shivering.

"It'll be exciting to see them in real life," said Micah. "They'll be friendly. They're only scary in the movies."

It might be fun to see their headdresses and war

paint from a distance. Maybe she could get a necklace. "Okay."

Micah pressed the button, and they tumbled into the fog and then blackness.

7

TAKING A SICK BABY TO HEAVEN

MICAH tumbled onto a braided carpet. It had a faint musty smell with a hint of dust. He glanced around. The room looked like an office. A large rolltop desk stood against one wall. On the other side of the room sat a long table with a tall wooden square set on top of it, divided into small sections, each about the size of an envelope. *Mail slots*, thought Micah.

Alicia lay in a crumpled heap beside him. "I wish just once we'd land on our feet or in a chair or on a soft bed. We're always dropping onto the ground—or in water."

Micah helped her up, and she brushed off her skirt.

Just then the door opened. In walked Brigham. "Well, here you are again." He gave them both a hug. "I'm guessing you didn't get home. I wish I could help you."

"Me too," said Micah.

"It's not that we don't like being with you," said Alicia. "But I miss my mom."

Brigham put his arm around her. "I know." He looked away. "I still miss mine."

Alicia hugged him.

"You've come on an exciting day," said Brigham. "I'm going to meet with Chief Walker, head of all the Indians in the area."

"Would you like to come along?"

"Sure," said Micah.

"Will the chief have on war paint and feathers?" asked Alicia.

Brigham laughed. "Who knows? Sometimes he wears them and sometimes he doesn't. I can never guess what mood he'll be in." Brigham shuffled some papers on his desk and put several letters in one of the mail slots. "The carriage is around front." He opened the door for Alicia and Micah.

The buggy waited on the street; the horses pawed the ground and nodded their heads. But the driver held the reins firmly.

"This is my son, Don Carlos," Brigham said, "one of my best drivers."

"Hello," said Don Carlos.

"Several months ago, he decided to skip school and ride with the men who drove my wagons," said Brigham.

Don Carlos rolled his eyes. "Father loves to tell this story."

"Well, then, you tell it," laughed Brigham.

Don Carlos smiled at his father. Micah could tell he loved Brigham.

"When Father heard that I kept skipping school," said Don Carlos, "he took me out of school and directly to the barn, where he gave me a pair of blind mules hitched to a wagon. He had me deliver vegetables and ice around the city. It was very hard work, with blind mules."

"The mules really couldn't see?" asked Micah. "How could you drive them?"

"I had to guide them carefully," said Don Carlos, "or they would run into things."

"I'll bet that was hard," said Alicia. "Was your father angry because you skipped school?"

"No," said Don Carlos. "I knew he wanted me to be the best at whatever I chose to be. And I loved driving the teams, so I worked hard to become the best."

He must like hard work, thought Micah.

"Now he's a very good driver," said Brigham. "Last week he took a load of wheat to Logan, eighty miles away."

"But I've decided to go back to school," said Don Carlos. "I want to become an architect, so I'm going to start at the University of Deseret here in Salt Lake City and then go back east to finish my studies."[1]

"Wow," said Alicia. "That's neat that your father let you do that."

"Neat?" said Don Carlos. "There wasn't anything messy about it."

Alicia giggled and covered her mouth. "It's just a saying we have. I should say, 'It's good your father let you do that.'"

Brigham laughed and patted Alicia's shoulder. "Come, we can't keep Chief Walker waiting."

Don Carlos drove the carriage out of the city to the surrounding hills. Teepees dotted the landscape to the left. As they drew closer, a tall, stately Indian with a full-feathered headdress hanging down his back rode his horse to the edge of the camp and stopped.

"The headdress is beautiful," said Alicia. "No war paint, so I hope he won't attack us."

"He's friendly," said Brigham.

"Is that Chief Walker?" asked Micah, watching the feathers on the headdress dance in the breeze.

Brigham nodded.

"Hello," called Brigham, when they drew near.

Don Carlos stopped the carriage when they reached the chief and helped his father to the ground. The chief dismounted and shook Brigham's hand in greeting.

"We've brought you some gifts," Brigham said to Chief Walker.

Don Carlos and Brigham began unloading blankets, clothes, and sacks of corn out of the back of the carriage.

"We always bring the Indians presents," said Brigham. "The Saints have moved into their land and taken over. Many of the Indians don't understand that we want to be friends. They just know that we catch the fish in their streams and eat their elk and deer in the winter.

"Sometimes they steal our horses and cattle because they're used to taking whatever they find in the wilderness, but we are still kind to them. It would cost more to buy bullets to fight them than to give them food and clothing. And after all, they are descendants of Book of Mormon people."[2]

Micah picked up a basket of clothing, and so did

Alicia. They carried them into camp. Women stood near their tents, watching, and dark-haired children hid behind them.

When the gifts were unloaded, Chief Walker and Brigham walked toward the fire. Teepees surrounded the area, with dark faces peering out of each of them.

"I need help," said Chief Walker.

"What's wrong?" asked Brigham.

"Sick child, close to death," said the chief. "Medicine man say he will die. I need someone to walk with him to the afterlife."

"What do you mean?" asked Brigham.

"Kill a white man to go with him to the spirit world."

Brigham looked shocked.

"Maybe this boy," said Chief Walker, pointing to Don Carlos, "or this girl." The chief pointed to Alicia. "Pretty necklace for you." He pulled a necklace out of his pocket and handed it to Alicia.

Alicia put her hands behind her back and shook her head no. "I don't want to take a sick baby to heaven."

"Don't kill her," said Micah, pulling Alicia toward him. Fear twisted his stomach. "It's all my fault that she's here." He put his arms around her shaking body.

Brigham stood in front of Alicia and Don Carlos as if to protect them. "Wait," he said. "Let me see the baby."

"Maybe the baby's already dead," whispered Alicia to Micah. "I'll be next."

"No, you won't," said Micah, hugging her tight. "I won't let him hurt you."

Don Carlos whispered to Alicia and Micah.

"Father will keep us safe. He's good with the Indians. They just have strange ways of thinking sometimes."

A squaw came out carrying a bundle in a dusty blanket. A weak cry came from inside followed by a hacking cough.

"Not dead yet," whispered Alicia through chattering teeth.

"May I give the baby a blessing?" asked Brigham. Chief Walker nodded.

Brigham laid his hands on the tiny bundle and by the power of the priesthood blessed the baby to be healed. He also prayed that no others would get sick.

"Many Indian children have died from the measles—a white man disease. I think Father doesn't want any more illness," whispered Don Carlos.

When Brigham finished, the baby quit crying and fell asleep.[3]

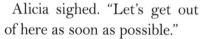

Alicia sighed. "Let's get out of here as soon as possible."

Another Indian walked up beside Chief Walker and put his hand on Brigham's shoulder. "What the other white men say go in one ear and out the other, but what Brigham say goes to the heart and stays there."[4]

"Thank you, Peteeneet," said Brigham. He turned

to Micah and Alicia. "This is Peteeneet, brother of Chief Walker."

"How do you do," said Micah.

Alicia backed away and didn't say anything.

Brigham helped Alicia and Micah into the carriage, and they waved good-bye.

"Well, that was an exciting day. Alicia, you almost got to go to heaven," Brigham teased.

Alicia put her hand on her hip. "That's not funny, Brigham. It was very scary."

Brigham hugged her. "I will keep you safe."

"Why are you so nice to the Indians?" asked Alicia. "The chief could have killed one of us."

"Some people say the Indians take advantage of you, Father," said Don Carlos.

"Maybe they do," said Brigham. "But when I meet Heavenly Father, I can tell Him I was kind to all His children."

"Are you nice to them so they'll join the Church?" asked Micah.

"Some of them may join the Church and some may not," said Brigham. "I want to be nice to them no matter what. Many of them don't want change. They love the traditions of their fathers. White man ways are not for them, and that's fine with me. I just want to live in peace."

The sun set as they reached the outskirts of the city. Micah glanced at Don Carlos. He and Alicia needed to be alone to try to get home, but he didn't want to tell Don Carlos. Brigham would understand. "This is a good place to meet our family," said Micah. "Thanks for a day with the Indians."

"Don't you want to come back to the house?" asked Don Carlos.

"They need to find their parents," said Brigham. "Stop the carriage." He turned to Micah and Alicia. "If things don't work out, you're always welcome at my house."

"Thanks," said Alicia. "Good luck becoming an architect, Don Carlos."

They climbed down from the carriage and waved until it was out of sight. Micah pulled the phone out of his pocket and swiped FUTURE.

TEXTING JOURNAL appeared.

"Let me type first," said Alicia. "I'm excited to say 'I didn't feel sorry for myself.' I guess I was too busy being afraid." She typed:

INDIAN WNTD ME TO GO TO HVN WITH SICK BABY.

SCRD, SCRD, SCRD. THX 4 LIFE! NO NEKLACE, NO SRY 4 SELF.

"I'm sorry I took Dad's phone," said Micah. "I'm sorry that seeing the Indians was frightening for you."

Micah typed:

INDIANS WNTD TO KILL ALICIA. BRGHM BLSSD BABY. IT GOT WELL.

NEVER TAKE FONE AGAIN, GUILT, THX ALICIA SAFE, WNT 2 GO HME.

FUTURE EVENTS lit the screen.

BRIGHAM BUILDS A HOME

WORK ON THE SALT LAKE TEMPLE BEGINS

MORMON WAR

"I don't want to see any fighting," said Alicia. "Today was scary enough."

SALT LAKE THEATER BUILT

BRIGHAM BUILDS A GYM FOR HIS CHILDREN

"I wish home was on the list," said Micah. "How will we ever get there?"

"Maybe we're stuck here for good." Alicia sighed. "If we can't get home, let's go see Brigham's kids."

Micah pressed the button, and they tumbled into the darkness.

8

PIONEER PLAY

ALICIA plummeted onto a braided rag rug, landing on a dog's tail.

"Aaiii," yelped the dog and moved off the rug.

Alicia looked around. Micah was sprawled next to her. A hot stove loomed in front of them. Across the room was a wooden sink lined with metal. It had a water-pump handle. *This is a kitchen,* she thought. *Oh, how I wanted it to be home. Maybe we'll never get there.*

"Get out of my kitchen!" came a booming voice. An Indian woman with a long black braid down her back shook a wooden spoon at Alicia and Micah.

"We—we just want to see Brigham Young," said Alicia.

"Dining room. Ten o'clock breakfast," said the woman, shooing them out of the kitchen and into the hall. "He coming soon."

Where is the dining room? Alicia wondered. She had no idea. A tall clock in the hall chimed ten times. She looked in each room as she walked. Micah followed.

One room had sofas and love seats and a piano. *That must be the living room,* thought Alicia. *Did they call it a parlor in the old days?*

She recognized the next room. "That's the office we landed in before going to see the Indians."

The following room had a long dining table. Alicia peeked her head in the door. A girl about her age sat at one end, swinging her legs back and forth.

"Hi," Alicia said.

"Hello," said the girl. "Who are you?"

"We're friends of Brigham's—uh, Brother Young's."

"Come in and wait with me," said the girl. "He's coming soon. My name is Clarissa, and everyone calls Father President Young, but Father doesn't care what you call him."

Red crept up into Alicia's neck and face. She should have known. "Sorry, I'll call him President Young."

Breakfast was spread for Brigham and Clarissa. Cornmeal mush, milk, hot doughnuts smothered in syrup, and fresh strawberries.

"Where are your parents?" asked Clarissa. "Did you just get here?"

"Yes," said Alicia. "We just got here." She didn't want to answer Clarissa's first question. It would get her into trouble.

"We're hopefully going to meet our parents a little later," said Micah.

Good answer, Alicia thought. She high-fived Micah in her mind.

Just then the opposite door to the dining room opened and in walked Brigham. "Alicia," he said, hugging her and slapping Micah on the back.

"Clarissa," said Brigham. "These are my friends, Alicia and Micah."

"Pleased to meet you," said Clarissa.

"Please sit down," said Brigham, sitting beside them. Before he began to eat, Clarissa tied a bib in the shape of a triangle over his long beard.

Alicia giggled. "That looks funny."

"To keep the crumbs away when I eat." Brigham smiled. "Clarissa, would you bless the food?"

"Yes, Father."

After the prayer, Brigham rang a bell. "I'll have Sally bring you some breakfast," Brigham said to Alicia and Micah.

The woman from the kitchen appeared at the door.

"This is Sally," said Brigham. "When she was a child, some Indians stole her from her parents and were going to take her to Mexico to sell her as a slave. Clara's brother found her, and Clara took her in. She's been part of the family ever since."[1] Brigham turned to Sally. "My young guests would like something to eat."

Sally frowned but was soon back with the same wonderful food Brigham and Clarissa ate.

"Yum," said Micah. He spooned some strawberries onto his plate and slid a doughnut on top of them.

Micah loves to eat, thought Alicia.

Brigham cleared his throat and looked at Alicia. "I'm sorry, but I've got other commitments today and can't spend time with you. I have meetings with the apostles, Governor Black, and Wilford Woodruff. He's the Church Historian, and we have some records to go over."

"It sounds like a busy day," said Alicia. "We don't want to bother you." She really wanted to get home and hang out with her friends, but it didn't look like that would happen.

"I have an idea," said Brigham. "Since today's Saturday and there's no school, Clarissa would be happy to show you around." He turned to Clarissa. "All right with you?"

"I'd love to, Father," said Clarissa, smiling.

"Great," said Micah with his mouth full of food. "Are there any boys around here?"

Brigham laughed. "Art, Clarissa's brother, is in the gym. She will find him."

Brigham turned to Clarissa. "Will you do that?"

"Yes, Father," said Clarissa.

Brigham finished his breakfast and hugged Clarissa. "I have to go."

She wrapped her arms around his neck and gave him a kiss. "Take off your beard napkin."

"Oh, I forgot," said Brigham, removing the cloth.

Alicia could tell Clarissa loved Brigham. Alicia wished she could hug her father.

"Tonight we'll all go to the theater to watch Clarissa dance."

Clarissa smiled and got up from her chair. "Let's go find Art."

"Just a minute." Micah shoved the last bite of doughnut in his mouth. "This is good," he mumbled as he chewed.

"You don't have to pig out," said Alicia.

"I'm hungry," said Micah.

"Pig out?" asked Clarissa. "There're no pigs here."

"Oh!" Alicia put her hands to her mouth. "I didn't mean pigs. It's just a saying."

"What do pigs have to do with your food?" giggled Clarissa.

"If you eat too much, like a pig, we say *pig out*," Alicia said. She had to watch her mouth.

"You must come from the south of England," said Clarissa. "People from the north wouldn't say that."

Alicia kept her mouth shut.

"Sometimes we all say silly things," said Clarissa.

When Micah finished, the three left the dining room.

"Let's go to the gym," said Clarissa. "I think I saw Art there earlier."

At the back of the house, Clarissa opened a door to a long room with a wooden floor. Along the walls were all kinds of equipment. There were ladders, skates, hoops, wooden swords, jump ropes and balls.[2] Children ran everywhere.

"Look at all these kids," Alicia whispered to Micah. "Where did they all come from?"

"Remember, they have polygamy," said Micah.

"Brigham has lots of wives and kids."

Clarissa waved to a tall, brown-haired boy lifting weights. He looked a little older than Micah. She motioned him over.

"Art, this is Micah," said Clarissa. "He's a friend of Father's, and he's here for the day. Father asked if you would show him around."[3]

"Nice to meet you," said Art. "I need to finish exercising. Come meet Albert and Alonzo. We're lifting barbells and then we're going to fence. When we're done, let's have a picnic down by the font."

"The font?" asked Micah.

"Oh." Clarissa giggled. "He means the swimming pool. That's what we call our pool because it's used for baptisms sometimes."

Alicia picked up a hoop. She lifted it over her head and swung it round her waist. She was never very good at hula-hooping, but maybe she could learn.

Clarissa began to laugh. "What are you doing?" she asked.

"Isn't this a hula hoop?" asked Alicia, feeling foolish.

"Hula? What's that," asked Clarissa. "I've never seen that done before. We roll the hoop along the ground with a stick, like this." She picked up a wand, shoved the hoop along the floor and ran after it, keeping it moving with the stick.

Alicia pulled the hoop back over her head and stood it up on the floor. It fell over.

"Push it ahead of you, like this," said Clarissa.

Alicia gave it a shove. The hoop wobbled and fell over again. "This is hard." She watched Clarissa, then pushed it ahead of her one more time, and it rolled along the floor. She ran to keep it going with her stick. Twice around the gym, and she stopped the hoop and put it in the box. She was out of breath from running. "That's hard," she puffed.

"Come meet some of my sisters," said Clarissa. "This is Charlotte, Josephine, and Ruth."

Alicia loved Charlotte's curly blonde hair. Josephine was tall and thin, and she could roll the hoop around the room very fast. Ruth's fair skin set off her dark hair and dark eyes.

The girls roller skated and jumped the rope. Clarissa showed Alicia how to jump with two ropes. Josephine and Clarissa were the best at it. She could see Micah and Art and the others fencing with wooden swords and later playing ball.

When the dinner bell rang for lunch, Alicia was surprised. Time had passed quickly.

"Mother's packed a lunch for the four of us to eat by the font," said Clarissa.

"What are we eating?" asked Micah.

Art looked in the dinner pail. "Bread, butter, and cheese with new carrots and popcorn for dessert. The font is just behind the schoolhouse. Not far."

A stream drifted into the pool at one end and rambled out the other side to meander through Brigham's orchard. They sat under a shade tree to eat. When they were finished, Art kicked his shoes off and ran and jumped in the water. Micah followed.

"Aren't they going to put on swimming suits?" asked Alicia.

"You mean suits for bathing?" asked Clarissa.

"Boys swim in their shirts and overalls," said Clarissa. "Girls wear linsey dresses. We have some in here." She opened the door of a small changing room. "This is an old bandwagon that Father made into a bathhouse."[4]

Alicia put on a plain cotton and wool dress Clarissa handed her.

"Wear these too," Clarissa said.

They looked like pants with ruffles around the ankles. "What are they?" asked Alicia, pulling them on. She felt like she was wearing a Mary-had-a-little-lamb costume. *I've never worn a bathing suit like this before*, she thought.

"They're pantalets," said Clarissa.

Mother is always talking about modesty, thought Alicia. *But this is over the top.* She walked out of the bathhouse dressed from her neck to her ankles. *I could never get a sun tan in this outfit.* She jumped into the water, and the wet dress and pan- talets hung heavy on her body. *How can anyone swim in this?* thought Alicia. *My swim team would laugh if they could see me now.* She tried a couple of "fly" strokes but couldn't get her arms out of the water in her linsey dress.[5]

They played the afternoon away, splashing each other, tossing their lunch bucket back and forth in a keep-away game, and floating on the water. As the sun slipped behind an apple tree in the backyard, the four of them got out, dried, and changed into fresh clothes before they went into the back of the house.

In the pantry, Art opened a cupboard and pulled out a bowl of candy. "This is stick jaw."[6] Art handed them each a piece.

"It looks like taffy," said Micah.

"It's like taffy, but it sticks your jaw together," laughed Clarissa. "We'll take some with us that you can eat while you watch my fairy dance."

"Great," said Alicia.

"Let's find Father," said Clarissa. "I have to leave for the theater before long."

The four of them walked outside and around to the front of the house, chewing their stick jaw. Brigham stood on the front steps talking to someone. He saw them and waved. Some other kids darted in and out across the lawn. It looked to Alicia like they were playing a game of tag.

"Come meet Brother Wilford Woodruff," called Brigham.

"President Woodruff," whispered Alicia to Micah. "Another prophet! Wow! That's amazing."

President Woodruff's beard was flecked with white, and it set off his square jaw. He carried a stack of notebooks.

"These are my friends, Alicia and Micah," said Brigham.

"It's nice to meet you," said President Woodruff. He shook Art's hand first and then the others'.

"Hello, Brother Woodruff," said Clarissa, tugging

her father's arm. "We need to get ready to go."

Brigham laughed. "She's a fairy in the production tonight."

"Well, you have important duties," said President Woodruff. "I'll take my leave."

Alicia stood with Micah, Art, Clarissa, and Brigham in front of the theater, waiting to go in.

"I'll take Clarissa back stage," said Brigham.

Clarissa juggled her dress and fairy wings from one arm to the other. She dropped one of her ballet slippers. Art picked it up and handed it to her.

"Good luck," said Alicia, waving as Clarissa walked toward the stage door. "Break a leg."

Clarissa stopped, turned, and looked at her. "Why would I want to break my leg?"

Alicia's face flushed pink. "I'm sorry. I didn't mean for you to really break your leg. It's just a saying when you're in a play that means good luck."

Alicia wasn't doing a very good job at watching her mouth. Her mother told her all the time that she had to think before she talked.

People lined up to pay for their tickets to the play. Some of them were holding animals. Alicia elbowed Micah. "Look," she giggled.

One man paid with a turkey and got two chickens for change.[7] The next woman paid with a squealing piglet. The following family carried a sack of wheat for their payment.

"Where are they putting all that stuff?" asked Micah.

"There's a room they keep it in," said Art.

Alicia wanted to ask why people didn't pay with money, but she knew Art would wonder where she came from, so she kept quiet.

Brigham came back to join them, talking with everyone along the way. When the theater doors opened, they went in. Candles gave the hall a soft glow. *No electric lights*, thought Alicia.

"My box is this way." Brigham led them to a special group of seats close to the stage that had a gate to keep them separate from the rest of the audience. Brigham opened the gate, and they went in. The stage lights were candles set in containers of sand. Alicia could see buckets of water waited just off stage.[8]

Micah saw them also. "I guess the water is in case of a fire."

After an opening prayer, the play began. Alicia loved watching Clarissa flit around the stage in her fairy costume. Alicia had taken dancing lessons when she was little, but now she liked her swim team better.

Being one of Brigham's children seemed fun. His life was so different from the young boy hacking bushes from the ground with no food to eat at home. Heavenly Father had really blessed him.

After the play, they met Clarissa and walked toward Brigham's home. Brigham held Alicia's hand and put his arm around Micah. "Did you have a good day?"

"Yes," said Micah, "but I have a question."

Alicia wondered what it would be. Micah was thinking about things, and that was good. Maybe he would come up with a way to get them home.

"What?" asked Brigham.

"This is the first day we've been with you that we didn't do any work. Even when we saw the Indians, we helped unload the gifts."

"Every day doesn't need to be a working day," said Brigham. "Saturday is a fun day. It's nice to have a good time once in a while. And then we always rest and attend our Church duties on the Sabbath."

"Father works us hard during the week," said Art. "After school, there are plenty of chores, like tending the animals and planting the garden or picking the fruit."

"Or building a new shed," said Brigham, "such as the one Art finished two days ago."

"Saturdays sound like the best," said Micah.

Brigham laughed. "They are. But I really like to work too." Brigham squeezed Alicia's hand.

Alicia knew her brother was getting better at working, and that was good.

Alicia looked at Micah and pulled at his shirt. "Let's go," she whispered. Out loud to everyone, she said. "Thanks for a fun day."

"But where are you going?" asked Clarissa. "You said you were meeting your parents."

"We are," said Micah.

"Stay with us," said Clarissa. "Your parents can live here also. We could be like sisters, Alicia."

"Not this time," said Brigham. "But they'll be back."

"I think you can count on it," sighed Micah.

Brigham smiled.

As they walked away, Alicia began to cry. After

seeing Brigham and his children together, she really missed her parents. "We're going to be stuck here forever. We started when Brigham was our age, and now his children are our age."

"I'm sorry I ever took Dad's phone," said Micah. "I want to get home too."

"I guess if we're going to be trapped in the past, this is as good a place as any," said Alicia. She started to cry harder. "Maybe we'll have to stay and be Brigham's children."

"Brigham is great," said Micah. "But we already belong to Mom and Dad. I want them for parents."

"So do I," said Alicia, tears dripping down her face. "So do I."

They sat on a wooden bench in front of a store that said "Zion's Cooperative Mercantile Institution."

"I don't feel like texting tonight," said Alicia.

"Me neither," said Micah, "but we have no choice."

"All right," said Alicia, grabbing the phone from Micah.

BRGHMS KIDS HAVE FUN HOME. WANT 2 B HOME, SRY 4 SELF!

"Is that it?" asked Micah.

"Yes," said Alicia. She pushed send.

Micah texted:

LRND 2 FENCE, SWAM IN A FONT. MAY B STUCK 4 EVER, GUILT.

I'M SRY ALICIA, WE NEED HLP.

He pushed send.

"I don't care where the phone takes us from here," said Alicia.

Micah pushed FUTURE rather than swiping it, and they tumbled into blackness.

9

THE PHONE
CRASHES

AS Micah fell from the sky, he saw a lake below him. Like a shooting star, he sped downward. *This is scary*, he thought. *The phone!* The phone couldn't get wet. He grabbed it from his pocket and hurled it toward the sandy shore with some black rocks in the background. He hoped it would land in the soft sand so it wouldn't crash and break. As he hit the water, salty brine shot into his nose and eyes. *Oh no*, he thought. *This is the Great Salt Lake. If the phone gets salt water in it, we're really dead!*

Stroking his hands to his sides to propel himself upward, he bobbed up like a buoy. He didn't need to kick his legs to stay afloat; he just sat in the water. Alicia yelled as she plunged in beside him.

He could see a group of people down the shore a ways. Was it Brigham? How would he explain falling out of the sky to them? He couldn't worry about that now; his first problem was to find the phone.

Scanning the shore in the direction he'd thrown the phone, he couldn't see it. His stomach lurched; it was full of swallowed salt water. He paddled toward the shore. The sting of brine bit into his eyes and nose, but it was easy to keep his head above water until he reached dry ground. Still no phone.

He heard Alicia slap at the water with her hand. "That's the second time I've landed in the water. Why can't we land someplace like a bed or sofa? What about the phone?" She yelled at Micah, "Did you let it get wet?"

His anger flared. Of course he didn't get it wet. He spun on his heels, facing Alicia in the hot afternoon sun. Squinting, he shouted back. "I threw the phone to the shore, and now I can't find it." He tightened his fists. Salt scratched at his skin like sandpaper. His jaw clenched, crunching salt between his teeth. Irritated, he spit. Salt was everywhere.

His wet shoes crackled across the salty sand on the shore. He took a deep breath. No point in letting his temper get the best of him. He wasn't really annoyed at Alicia anyway. He was angry at himself. His feelings prickled inside his body like the gritty salt that covered him.

He looked around again. Where did the phone land? Now he was really worried. What if they couldn't find it?

Alicia reached the shore. "I'll help you look."

"I think I threw it near here," said Micah.

"There." Alicia pointed and ran to an outcropping of black rock.

Micah rushed to her side. The phone lay in pieces. The back had popped off, and the battery stuck out of a small crack in the rock.

Alicia shoved her hair out of her face. "What'll we do? It's broken, so now we're really stuck here for good."

Micah tightened his fists. "I guess we are." This whole mess was all his fault. He felt so guilty. He would stay here for the rest of his life and take his punishment. But Alicia didn't deserve to lose her life and her family forever. He smacked one fist into his other hand. *Why did I think going to the future would be cool?*

Micah swiped his hands on his pants to get the salt off. It clung to him. Scraping his hands against the rock cleaned them a little better.

He picked up the phone by the edges.

"Can you put it back together?" asked Alicia.

Micah turned the phone over and snapped the battery in. He tried to lock the back on. "The clasp is broken. The back won't stay."

He held it together firmly and touched the screen. No light—the phone was dead.

"What are we going to do?" asked Alicia. "We'll never get home."

Reality set in. They were never going home. Before he had hope, but not now. "I'll think of something," said Micah, trying to be positive. He didn't want Alicia to be discouraged.

Shouts from the water caught Micah's attention. He turned to see a paddle-wheel boat.

"Is that Brigham and Clarissa?" asked Alicia. "And Charlotte, I think."

"I see Art too."

As the boat neared the shore, Micah could see a

horse walking a treadmill at the back. *That must be what makes the paddle wheel go around*, thought Micah. He hid the phone behind his back. He didn't want to put it in his pocket and get it all wet.

"Hello," called Brigham as he slid large wooden boards from the ship to the shore and then walked down the planks. He put his arm around Alicia, and she started to cry. "What's wrong?"

"We can't ever get back home," she said.

Brigham hugged her. "I'm sorry. It wouldn't be so bad for you to stay with me, would it?"

Alicia shut her eyes.

"I'd like to help, but I don't know what to do," said Brigham. "You can be part of my family until you figure out how to get home. I'd love that. In fact, I feel like you practically belong to the Young family anyway."

Micah knew Alicia wanted her own mother and father, not Brigham, even though she liked him a lot.

"Thanks," said Micah, blinking back his own tears. "Thanks."

Brigham looked down at their clothes. "How did you get all wet? You must have landed in the water." He turned to Alicia. "At least it's not as dangerous as the river was. You're all salty. We have some dry clothes on board."

Micah glanced at the group of people swimming further down the lake shore. "Are they part of your family?" he asked.

"That's Brother Grant. He brings his family here quite often," said Brigham. "They live out here near the lake." Brigham turned back to the boat. "Clarissa and Charlotte, bring some clothes for Alicia and Micah."

"Hello." Clarissa waved. "How did you get here? Did you come with the Grants? I see them swimming down the shore. I'm glad you're here. I'll be right there with some dry things and two towels."

"I hope she doesn't ask us again how we got here," said Micah to Alicia.

"I'm not going to tell her anything unless she asks," said Alicia. "Remember what trouble we had explaining the phone to Brigham."

"I don't want to do that again," said Micah.

Soon Clarissa came ashore with Art and Charlotte behind her.

"When we go swimming, we always change behind that big black rock." Clarissa pointed. "Father says girls on one side and boys on the other."[1]

Alicia went around one side of the rock and Micah took the other side.

Micah hoped Clarissa would forget about asking where he and Alicia came from. He brushed himself hard with the towel to get the salt off. The clean shirt and overalls felt fresh. Their stiffness meant they were dried in the sunshine like the time their electric dryer broke down. They weren't soft like the clothes just out of the dryer at home. He carefully stuffed the phone in his pocket. He'd look at it later. Maybe he could get it working.

"Nice boat," Micah said to Art. Micah held his breath. Would Art ask how he and Alicia got there?

"Father had it built," said Art. "He named it 'Timely Gull.'"[2]

"Do you just leave the horse on it?" asked Micah.

"No," Art laughed. "Father will get the horse to help pull our wagon home."

The wagon jolted over ruts in the dirt road. Dust sifted up and into Micah's mouth, mixing with the left-over salt. Yuck.

Clarissa and Charlotte chattered about school and a new quilt Clarissa's mother had just finished with a log cabin pattern.

How do you put log cabins on a quilt? wondered Micah. It sounded confusing to him.

Alicia sat quietly listening. *She must be sad*, thought Micah. He was glad no one had asked where they came from. He breathed a sigh of relief. Maybe they were safe from explaining.

"And Father gave us each a new ten cent bill after family prayer the other night,"[3] said Clarissa. "Some of the family missed prayer, and they were upset because they didn't get a bill. I'm so glad I went to family prayer. I'm going to try to be there every night."

Micah wondered if he could talk his parents into giving him money if he came to family prayer. *Probably not a good idea*, he thought.

"Father," said Art when they reached the city limits, "drive past the temple. I want Micah to see how high the walls are."

"You know I always love to show off the temple," said Brigham. He turned left and drove past some houses until he reached the temple grounds. He pulled the wagon to a halt. A few men worked with chisels on the stone walls. Others stood on scaffolding, measuring and talking together. Oxen lumbered by, dragging a large granite stone entangled in a huge web of ropes.

Micah felt a reverence on the temple grounds. Even though men were busy hammering and calling to each other, they seemed happy. He could feel peace; it seemed to blanket the entire temple grounds.

The walls of the temple were partway up. Stones fitted into the beginnings of round, empty circles. Micah knew that was where the round windows would go. He'd seen the finished temple. It was weird to see the building only partway done when Micah had seen it completed. He looked around Temple Square. The tabernacle was there, but it didn't have a shiny roof. Seagull Monument hadn't been built. He and Alicia liked to play in the water around it. There were no green shade trees or pretty flowers. The temple and tabernacle grounds were just dirt.

"Father wants the temple to be perfect," said Art. "One day he saw the workers putting granite shavings in between the stone blocks rather than cement. He made them take it out and start again."[3]

"This temple will stand through the Millennium," said Brigham.[4] "And someday there will be hundreds of temples all over the earth."[5]

"There are temples all over—" Alicia started to say.

Micah put his hand over Alicia's mouth. "Shhhh," he whispered. "Maybe Brigham doesn't know yet."

"Maybe he saw it in a vision, so he does know," whispered Alicia.

Micah wondered if the baptismal font in this temple would have twelve oxen holding it up like the one in his temple where he did baptisms for the dead.

At dinner that night, Micah was hungry but couldn't eat. Worry choked his throat. Art sat next to him tanking down his mashed potatoes and gravy. It looked good. Micah just couldn't eat. He watched Alicia push her food around her plate. She sat with Clarissa, Ruth, Josephine, and Charlotte. *It must be fun to be part of a big family like this. You'd always have friends.* They helped clear the table after dinner.

The smooth tones of a bell floated through the house. Everyone left what they were doing and hurried down the hall. Micah heard the patter of children's small feet, skipping from every direction, followed by more grown-up footsteps. The family met in the parlor.

"What are they doing?" Micah asked Art.

"It's seven o'clock. Time for family prayer," said Art. "Come on."

Micah followed him into the room. Alicia was already there. She hurried to his side, taking his hand and standing very close to him.

Clara Young pulled them near her. "Sit here by my family."

Micah and Alicia settled next to Clara.

Brigham sat in a large chair; a small leather-bound book lay open in his hands. Candles flamed from brass candlesticks, giving the room a golden glow.[6]

Brigham spoke. "Tonight I'd like to read to you from the Doctrine and Covenants. Remember, Oliver Cowdery wrote as Joseph translated the Book of Mormon. Oliver wanted to translate from the golden plates too, so Heavenly Father told him he could. Oliver tried, but he couldn't do it. The Lord told him, "Behold, you have not understood; you have supposed that I would give it unto you, when you took no thought save it was to ask me. But behold, I say unto you, that you must study it out in your mind; then you must ask me if it be right, and if it is right I will cause that your bosom shall burn within you; therefore, you shall feel that it is right."[7]

Brigham closed his Doctrine and Covenants and looked directly at Micah. "Now I know some of you have problems you need to work through, and I promise you that if you study your problems out in your mind and ask the Lord, He will help you figure out what to do and bless you."

Micah gazed into Brigham's blue eyes. He hadn't said anything to Brigham about the broken phone and being stuck for good, but Brigham knew. Micah hung his head. He and Alicia hadn't prayed about getting home. Micah had relied on his own knowledge and tried to solve the problem himself. He'd gotten nowhere because he needed to include the Lord. Then maybe he and Alicia would get back to their family.

Micah squeezed Alicia's hand. She squeezed back. She knew too.

The family sang "Praise to the Man." Micah watched Brigham sing. He knew Brigham loved Joseph Smith. Maybe he was thinking of the day they met the prophet together. Micah thought about Joseph Smith's clear eyes and strong testimony. At the end of the song, Brigham said, "I feel like shouting Hallelujah all the time when I think that I ever knew Joseph Smith."[8]

The family knelt, and Brigham began to pray. He asked Heavenly Father to bless the Saints and his family, including Micah and Alicia. Micah thought it felt good to have a prophet pray for him.

After prayer, everyone rose.

"One more thing," said Brigham. "Tomorrow morning, we leave for St. George and will visit the Saints along the way. Those of you who are coming, be ready by 8 a.m. I want to spend some time with the people in St. George."

Micah caught Brigham's eye. "Thanks," he said.

Brigham smiled at him.

Micah took Alicia by the arm. "Let's go out by the swimming pool where we can be alone and pray. I really want to get us home."

"I do too," said Alicia. "I have to tell Heavenly Father we're sorry we haven't been praying about getting home."

They walked in silence. The clouds on the western hills turned pink in the last rays of the setting sun.

"Do you think prayer will zap the phone problems away?" asked Alicia

"No," said Micah. "Remember what Brigham said, 'We still have to study it out in our minds and then ask Heavenly Father.'"

"If I could text right now, I would promise to keep a prayer in my heart always," said Alicia. "But I don't know what we need to do differently so the phone will take us home."

"Me neither," said Micah.

"Let's find someplace to pray now," said Alicia.

Micah led the way to the swimming pool behind the schoolhouse. The sound of rushing water seemed to calm him. They knelt under an apple tree.

"Heavenly Father, please help us get home," pleaded Micah. "Please tell us how to fix the phone."

After the prayer, they sat under the tree. Dimming daylight ghosted the moon into the coming dark. He pulled the phone out of his pocket and made sure the battery was locked in before he pressed the back firmly against it.

Alicia swiped the screen. It remained black. "Take the battery out again and look at it more closely."

Micah did. He noticed the memory chip wasn't snapped in place. He fixed it and put the phone back together. He swiped the screen—nothing. He pressed the back more firmly. The screen flickered. He moved his thumb a little to the side, and the phone lit up.

PAST

PRESENT

FUTURE

"It worked," said Micah. "I guess 'studying it out' means to try to figure out what to do."

"We prayed and thought about it, and Heavenly Father blessed us to know what to do."

I'm thankful for His help, thought Micah.

"He does answer our prayers," said Alicia.

Micah swiped FUTURE.

TEXTING JOURNAL REQUIRED

Alicia typed:

LANDED IN THE GRT SLT LK, PRYD 2 GT HME

<3 2 B HOME, MISS U MOM & DAD, ALWS PRY IN MY <3.

Micah typed:

BRGHM HAS A BOAT PWRD BY HORSE. SAW SL TEMPLE NT FNSHD.

PRY, PRY, PRY. THX HVNLY FTHR ANSR 2 PRYR—FONE WRKD.

A list of events appeared.

BRIGHAM VISITS THE SAINTS IN LEHI, PROVO, SPANISH FORK

BRIGHAM "KIDNAPS" THE BRASS BAND FROM NEPHI

"How fun is that," said Alicia. "I'd like to go there."

"I thought you wanted to get home," said Micah.

"I do," said Alicia, shaking her head. "What was I thinking? Take us home."

BRIGHAM VISITS SETTLEMENTS IN CENTRAL UTAH

BRIGHAM OVERSEES THE TEMPLE IN ST. GEORGE

ST. GEORGE TEMPLE DEDICATION

BRIGHAM YOUNG'S DEATH

"It's the end of his life, and there is no button for home," said Micah.

"Prayer helped us figure out how to fix the phone. But now what?"

"I guess go to St. George and keep praying. Maybe we'll find some help there."

Micah swiped, and blackness enveloped them.

10

BUILDING
THE TEMPLE

ALICIA landed in a hill of dirt. She slid off the pile onto crunchy black gravel. Shaking her long, blue dress and stomping off her stiff leather shoes reminded her that she wasn't home yet. She ran her fingers through her hair and pulled it back, putting the bonnet hanging around her neck up over her head to protect her face from the sun. She was upset. Even after praying, they weren't home. Was Heavenly Father even listening?

Micah rolled over next to her. Alicia watched him dig dirt out of his left ear. He squeezed the phone between his thumb and forefinger. It lit.

ST GEORGE, UTAH, DECEMBER 31, 1876.

Alicia glanced at it. "Why didn't prayer take us home?"

"I don't know," said Micah. "And I don't know what to do."

"Nothing is working," said Alicia.

"All we can do is pray some more," said Micah.

"I will," said Alicia. "But it doesn't seem to be help-ing." The sun glared in her face. "It's hot here—even in December."

"These black rocks seem hotter than regular rocks." Micah sneezed. "And dusty too."

"At least it's not salt water this time," said Alicia. She'd hated the stiff sandy feeling of the salt all over her when she got out of the Great Salt Lake. She looked around. They stood on a hill covered with crusty black rock. There were no trees. She could see little stone houses and log cabins in the distance. Turning around, she saw the temple looming up in front of her. Alicia looked at the white building glistening in the sun. Workmen carried the scaffolding away from the lower part of the temple while plasterers painted the red sandstone blocks a shining white.

"Hello there," called a man standing by a wagon full of dirt. The small donkey in front of the cart flicked its ears and let out a loud hee-haw.

Alicia glanced around. No one else was close. The man must be talking to them.

He walked over. "I'm President Erastus Snow.[1] You must be some of the Saints who have traveled from a great distance to help on the temple."

"Hello," said Micah. "We're Micah and Alicia."

"Does your family need us to find you a place to stay?"

"No thanks," said Micah, glancing at Alicia.

President Snow patted Micah on the shoulder. "Well, we appreciate you coming to help. Pick up those shovels and spread the dirt around. We've got to get this ground ready to plant grass and trees for the temple dedication."

Micah pulled a shovel from the hill of dirt and handed it to Alicia.

President Snow smiled and walked back to his cart.

"Work again," Micah said to Alicia. "I still don't love it. Maybe helping on the temple will be different than regular work." He grabbed a spade for himself.

Alicia hoped Micah would learn to enjoy work like she did. But he never felt sorry for himself. That was what she needed to work on.

President Snow snatched his own shovel and began to unload dirt off the cart. He broke into song. "The spirit of God like a fire is burning. The latter-day glory begins to come forth . . ."

A horse clip-clopped near, drawing a carriage. "Alicia and Micah?"

Alicia turned. "Brigham!" The driver stopped the buggy.

"Climb up here and let me give you a hug," said Brigham.

Brigham had a few more wrinkles in his face now, and his hair and beard were flecked with white.

"It's good to see you two again." He turned to the man singing. "This is President Erastus Snow."

"We've already met," said President Snow, laughing heartily. "And I've put them to work." He helped Micah and Alicia up into the carriage.

Turning back to his load of dirt, President Snow went on with his song while he shoveled. "The visions and blessings of old are returning."

Alicia put her arms around Brigham. Her head
nestled into the soft beard, resting on his chest. "It's
nice to see you," she said. Alicia had never been in a
carriage before. She gave a little bounce on the soft
black leather seat. It let out a squeak and jiggled a
little.

"I'm glad you're here," said Brigham. "I want to
show you the temple." The driver urged the horses
forward.

Alicia looked up at the temple. In the sunshine,
light seemed to be glowing from the building. Her
breath caught in her throat. "The temple looks like a
castle that floated down from heaven."

Brigham smiled at her. "It's built to give our families heavenly gifts." He used his cane to push himself forward in his seat. "I'm anxious to see that my
father and mother are baptized and that we're sealed
together as a family before I die."[2]

Oh, thought Alicia, feeling sad. *I wish he wasn't old.*

"I want the temple finished as soon as possible. I
need to give others the sealing power that I have so
every family can be together forever."[3]

Our family is a together-forever family, thought
Alicia, feeling happy inside.

The buggy passed the steps leading up to the two
large front doors of the temple. "I have to go in a side
door," said Brigham. "I can't walk up the steps."

As the carriage stopped, several workmen hurried
to help Brigham out of the buggy. They set him on a
chair to carry him into the temple.

He really can't walk, thought Alicia. She watched
the muscles in Brigham's face tighten as the men lifted

him. *He must be in pain.* She held her breath as they took him to the building. She hoped he didn't hurt too much.

How could she feel sorry for herself about not getting home when Brigham was in real pain and still had a temple to build?

The men took Brigham through the open door and set him down.

As Alicia stepped inside the temple, cool air wafted over her. It began to dry the sweat on her forehead.

"You're here just in time," said Brigham. "Tomorrow, on New Year's Day, we're dedicating the baptismal font, first floor and a few sealing rooms of the temple."

"Oh," said Alicia, "a temple dedication. Can we come?"

"Of course. I want you to come." Brigham winced as he settled into his chair.

"What's the matter with your legs?" asked Alicia.

"It's my rheumatism," said Brigham. "I'm getting old, and I don't feel very well."

A short man with a broad forehead and round face approached Brigham. "President, how are you today?"

Brigham smiled and shook his hand. "Brother Angell, this is Micah and Alicia, friends of mine. Brother Angell is the architect of this beautiful temple."[4]

"Hi," said Micah.

"Hello," said Alicia.

"Brother Angell, would you show them around the temple? I'm in too much pain to do it today."

"With pleasure," said Brother Angell. "Can I get you anything before we go?"

"No, just let me rest. It comforts me to be in the House of the Lord."

Brother Angell directed Alicia and Micah down the hall toward some steps leading down to the basement. "Let's start with the baptistery."

In the basement, they walked through a dressing area into a large room. It was all white with a big shiny font that looked like a bowl cradled on the back of twelve oxen. Wrought iron stairs led up into the font on either side, and a white wrought iron railing surrounded the circular platform above the oxen.

"Oh," breathed Alicia. "It's beautiful. I feel so happy here."

"The baptismal font in our temple looks almost exactly like this," said Micah.

"What?" asked Brother Angell. "Which temple is that?" Brother Angell looked at Micah. "You mean the Nauvoo Temple?"

"Ah," stammered Micah. He coughed. "Er . . ." His face turned red.

Alicia kicked his ankle and rolled her eyes. *Both of us have trouble keeping our mouths shut,* she thought.

"Come see the endowment room." Brother Angell led them back upstairs into a large room with carpet on the floor and paintings on the walls—a lamb and a lion resting side by side, hillsides covered with trees and flowers, and a bird in flight.

"This is like being in the middle of a picture," said Alicia.

Brother Angell laughed. "We have wonderful artists from Norway and Denmark. They have worked for months on these murals."[5]

Only three of the stairs up to the next floor were completed. "How can the dedication be tomorrow?" asked Alicia. "The temple isn't finished."

"All the carpenters are working long hours, but the entire building won't be completed for about three or four months," said Brother Angell.

"Can we help?" asked Alicia, glancing at Micah.

Micah looked at her, shaking his head no.

Alicia turned quickly as if she hadn't seen Micah's signal. She didn't care if he wouldn't work. She wanted to help. "I can help outside spreading dirt and planting flowers."

"If you want to," said Brother Angell, "but many of the women and young girls are making beautiful rag rugs to go on the floor."

"I can do that if someone shows me how," said Alicia.

"Wonderful," said Brother Angell. "We'll use all the help we can get."

Alicia smiled at Micah. He didn't really like work yet.

"Come tomorrow to the dedication and listen to President Young speak. He has a wonderful way of teaching us the things we need to know."

Alicia felt very excited to go to the first temple dedication in the Utah territory—especially to be there with Brigham. But would he be able to stand and give his speech?

That evening, Micah and Alicia sat outside in the garden with Brigham.

"Thanks for letting us stay with you," said Alicia.

"You know I love having you," said Brigham, "even though you want to get home."

"I've been wondering," said Micah, "why Heavenly Father hasn't answered our prayers. We don't know what else to do to get home."

Brigham leaned back in his chair and gazed toward the sunset. "Remember Enos. He prayed 'mightily' to the Lord, and he kept praying until he got an answer to his prayer. So, 'study it out in your mind' like Oliver Cowdery did and continue to pray, and Heavenly Father will answer you. Just be patient."[6]

"We'll keep working on it," said Micah.

That night Micah and Alicia texted their journal even though they weren't going anywhere.

Micah typed:

SEE THE ST. GEORGE TMPL, BPTSML FONT LIKE OLD TSTAMNT ONE.

PRAY TO GET HME. TSTIMNY, WRK ON TMPL.

Alicia typed:

ST. GEORGE TMPL LOOKS LIKE A CASTLE FROM HVN.

BRGHM CAN'T WALK.

THX 4 WRK ON TMPL, THX 4 PRYR. PRY, PRY, PRY, <3
HME.

11

DEDICATION
TO THE LORD

MICAH sat with Alicia near the front of the assembly room where the dedication would take place. Many Saints arrived early and talked quietly in their seats. Brigham's daughter Susa Gates had brought them early so they would get a good seat. She sat with them now, waiting for the meeting to start.

"I love the baptismal font," said Alicia.

"It is beautiful," said Susa. "Before the men began work on it, Father had me read to him the descriptions of the tabernacle in Leviticus, and Solomon's temple in Chronicles and Kings. He wanted to make sure the font was like the one in Solomon's temple."[1]

When I go to do baptisms for the dead, I'll remember that Brigham made the font like the ones in the Old Testament, thought Micah. "President Young seemed so happy at breakfast this morning," he said out loud. "I'm glad he can dedicate this temple."

All of a sudden, the chatter in the room ceased. Quiet crept over the audience. Some men in suits entered the room, followed by a group of brethren carrying Brigham in a chair. Everyone stood.

Micah felt the room fill with the Spirit. He stood very still—afraid even a movement might disrupt the feeling. He would remember this moment forever.

Elder Wilford Woodruff spoke, and then Brigham Young Jr., and finally President Erastus Snow. Then a hush came over the Saints and everyone looked to Brigham. Micah watched him struggle to his feet.

Brigham rose—when he couldn't even walk a little while ago. *A miracle*, thought Micah. Brigham's face shone with light. He made his way carefully to the pulpit. As he began to speak, his voice filled the room.[2]

"When I think upon this subject [temple blessings], I want the tongues of seven thunders to wake up the people,"[3] Brigham said.

"Can the fathers be saved without us? No. Can we be saved without them? No."[4]

There was a pause, and then he continued. "Are you satisfied now that the temple is finished?" Brigham asked. "I am not half satisfied until I have whipped . . . the devils from this earth."[5]

Micah watched Brigham raise his cane and smash it down on the podium.

Crack!

Micah jumped. Others did too. Then no one moved. As Brigham put his cane back on the floor, Micah could see two dents in the pulpit from the knots in Brigham's cane.[6]

Something happened inside Micah. Tears filled his eyes. He felt different—stronger than before. He knew Brigham was a prophet of God, and he was grateful that he, plain everyday Micah, was friends with a prophet.

Micah thought about getting home and knew Heavenly Father would help him figure it out. Happiness and love filled him until he felt like bursting or floating up to the ceiling.

Alicia leaned over and whispered to him, "We're going to be okay. I know Heavenly Father will help us get home." Micah knew she felt it too.

Brigham hobbled back to his chair, and the congregation sang, "The Spirit of God like a fire is burning." Micah remembered when he was little thinking this was the "fire burning" song. He didn't understand why they would sing a song about fire at church. But now that he was older, he understood. The music filled him with the Spirit. Being in the temple was so wonderful he didn't want to leave. Maybe he could talk Alicia into staying in St. George for a little while so they could work on the temple. He loved the feeling he got here. He wondered if he could keep the same feeling with him when he got home.

After the dedication, Micah pulled Alicia aside. "I loved the meeting today. I know Brigham is a prophet and the work on the temple is really important."

"I loved the meeting too," said Alicia.

"Now that the Spirit has told us we're going to get home, I want to stay for a little while and help finish the temple. I want to keep the feeling I have."

"I don't know," said Alicia. "I've been wanting to get home for so long." She was quiet for a minute. "Mom and Dad are probably going crazy because we've been gone for so long."

"If they know we're gone, I'll bet they miss us," said Micah.

"I think they're probably very upset," said Alicia. "Maybe we should go back."

"We don't know how this time travel works," said Micah. "Maybe we're moving forward in time here, but at home it's standing still." He wished Alicia would say yes. "I really want to stay."

Alicia sighed. "Well, I want to stay too and keep the feeling I've had today. I know that sounds weird because I've been so homesick and worried about getting back." She smiled. "I hope Mom will be okay if we stay and help finish the temple."

"Heavenly Father will bless us if we do His work," said Micah.

He was glad Alicia wanted to stay. They both felt the Spirit.

That evening after the dedication, the sun nestled itself into the red hills in the west. The garden behind Brigham's house cooled in the shade of a mulberry tree. Brigham sat in a large, wooden lawn chair, and Micah and Alicia rocked in a pine swing big enough for four people.

"I suppose you'll try again to get back home," said Brigham.

"I—I was wondering if we could stay and help finish the temple," said Micah.

Alicia sat forward on her chair. "This morning at the dedication when you were speaking, I felt so happy inside. I want to stay too."

Brigham's face lit up into a broad grin. "Well, then. It's settled. You can stay with me as long as you want."

"Thanks," said Micah.

"By the way," said Brigham. "I've been wondering about the magic tablet you have. I've seen you put it in your pocket a few times."

"I didn't know you saw me." Micah glanced over at Alicia with a guilty look. He hadn't kept it hidden very well.

"Show him," said Alicia.

Micah pulled the phone out of his pocket and explained it to Brigham the best he could.

"I'd like to come and see your lives in the future. There are such wonderful inventions. But I haven't got the energy. It's almost time for me to return to Heavenly Father."

The last rays of light burned the sky bright red like the hills.

"Tell me about your time," said Brigham.

"Well," said Alicia, "remember when you showed us the Salt Lake Temple? You said there would be hundreds of temples on the earth?"

"Yes," said Brigham.

"Well, there are over a hundred temples all over the earth now," Micah said.

Brigham smiled. "Isn't that glorious?"

"We've had many prophets since your time," said Alicia.

"There are members of the Church all over the world, and they can watch temple dedications from far away in their own churches on a big screen. They can also see conference, and read or listen to the prophet's talks on a computer," said Micah.

"I don't understand it all. It's a miracle—like the magic we called it when you first came to see me," said Brigham.

"It's kind of like magic to us too," said Micah. "I don't really know how a computer works even though I can use one."

"I'll just have to take your word for it," said Brigham. "How is the Salt Lake Temple now that it's finished?"

"It's wonderful," said Alicia. "I'm going there to do baptisms for the dead when I'm twelve."

"Great," said Brigham. "Are you praying about how to get home?"

"We're praying and trying to figure out what to do," said Alicia.

"I know Heavenly Father will help us," said Micah. "But for now we want to stay."

Micah and Alicia worked on the temple. Micah and others spread thousands of loads of dirt on the black volcanic rock around the grounds. His muscles ached. He planted flowers and dug holes for new trees. He loved working near President Snow, who sang. Micah sang right along with him, feeling happy while he worked.

Alicia made rugs with other girls her age. "I watch the girls and their mothers together, and I miss Mom," Alicia told Micah as they walked back to Brigham's house one day.

"I miss her and Dad too, but I'm happy we're here." Micah had just spread manure on all the flower beds.

The scent of the fertilizer filled his nose. He felt stinky.

Alicia combed her hair back with her fingers and put her bonnet back on her head. "I'm not going to feel sorry for myself. I've chosen to stay here for a little while, and I'm using my faith that Heavenly Father will bless us to get home. Tomorrow I'm going to help clean and polish the floors and railings in the new part of the temple."

Micah stretched his back as he walked. It ached.

"I wish we knew for sure that we were going to get back home when we're finished here," said Alicia. "Sometimes my faith is stronger than other times."

Micah and Alicia worked long hours. Micah sang with President Snow even when he was tired. Days turned into weeks. January, February, and March slipped by.

Soon it was the first of April, and the temple was finally finished. Micah, Alicia, and Brigham sat under the mulberry tree outside the summer kitchen of Brigham's home.

"I don't feel well," said Brigham. "I'm not as young as I used to be."

"I wish you felt better," said Alicia.

"Well," said Brigham, "you've watched my life from the time I was a poor farm boy until I became a prophet and helped settle the West. I can't take credit for all the things I have done. Heavenly Father made them all possible.

"It was the power of God . . . I could never have devised such a plan."[7]

"I've heard President Snow call you 'Lion of the Lord,'" said Micah.

"I want to be a Lion for the Lord," said Brigham. "The gospel . . . burned in my bones like fire pent up. . . . Nothing would satisfy me but to cry abroad in the world what the Lord is doing in the latter days."[8]

"We know you're faithful," said Micah. "I want to be that faithful and work hard for Heavenly Father also."

"You *have* worked hard for Heavenly Father, finishing this beautiful building," said Brigham. "Tomorrow we will dedicate the entire St. George Temple. Now everyone who is worthy can receive their temple blessings and return to Heavenly Father forever." Brigham looked at the setting sun. "In the Bible, the Savior told Peter He would give him the 'keys of the kingdom of heaven; and whatsoever thou shalt bind on earth shall be bound in heaven.'"[9]

"What does that mean?" asked Micah.

"It's the greatest blessing the Savior could give us. Every prophet who will ever live on the earth will have the keys of the sealing power to bind us as families so we can be together for eternity—forever and ever. And that happens only in the temple."

"I'm glad I'll be with my family forever," said Alicia.

"Me too," said Micah. "I think we'll try to get back home now that the temple is finished. We could stay for the dedication tomorrow, but I promised Alicia we'd get home as soon as we helped finish the temple."

"I really miss my mom," said Alicia. "But we'll be sad to leave you."

"I've loved having you around," said Brigham, struggling to his feet. "I hope you get home this time."

He rubbed his back. "My bones ache, so I'll say good night. Tomorrow will be a big day."

Susa came to help him into the house.

"Wait," said Alicia. She put her arms around Brigham and gave him a big hug. "I love you."

Brigham's eyes watered. "I love you too."

"Thanks for everything," said Micah, hugging him also.

"You've grown up," said Brigham.

Susa helped Brigham shuffle into the house.

12

HOME

MICAH and Alicia sat close together on the swing. Micah pulled the phone from his pocket and held it together with his thumb and forefinger. He swiped it, and it lit up.

PAST

PRESENT

FUTURE

"Before I press it, let's have a prayer," said Micah. "We're at the end of Brigham's life. We have to figure it out now. Alicia, will you pray that Heavenly Father will help us know what to do?"

Alicia prayed that they might be able to get home.

Micah looked at the phone again with a silent prayer still in his heart. An idea came into his head. He needed to press the PRESENT button this time and not the FUTURE. He looked at Alicia. "A thought just came into my head that I didn't think of myself. Does that sound too weird?"

"What is it?"

"I have a feeling I need to press PRESENT and not FUTURE. I don't know why."

"I was thinking that same thing—maybe the PRESENT button will get us back to our present time."

"It's like it wasn't my own thought," said Micah.

"Maybe it was the Holy Ghost telling you what to do," said Alicia.

"Maybe," said Micah. "All I know is I have to remember to pray, and Heavenly Father will help me. I like that feeling."

"Me too," said Alicia.

Micah pressed PRESENT. TEXTING JOURNAL lit the screen.

ST. GEORGE TMPL DONE. HLPD PLNT FLWRS & TREES.

THX 4 TSTIMNY, THX FOR BRGHM, THX FOR TMPLS, THX 4 HRD WRK.

He pushed send.

Alicia took the phone.

BRGHM LOVES THE TMPL, I LOVE IT TOO. I CAN MAKE RUGS!

THX FOR BRGHM, NO SRY 4 SELF, <3 U MOM & DAD, TSTIMNY.

She pushed send.

Blackness surrounded them and fog enveloped them. "The phone didn't tell us a specific place it would take us," said Alicia through the mist. "Home, home, home," she shouted.

When the haze cleared, they found themselves sitting on the rock in front of their house.

"You did it, Micah," gasped Alicia. "We're home."

Micah watched her twist her CTR ring on her finger and feel her necklace around her throat. He grabbed her hands.

Micah bowed his head, and Alicia did also. "Thanks, Heavenly Father. Thanks for the gift of the Holy Ghost. Thanks for getting us home." Micah closed his prayer and looked up smiling at Alicia. He gave her a hug.

Alicia grinned back and ran into the house. "Mom, Mom we're home."

Micah followed.

"That's nice," said her mother. "I'm just scrubbing the potatoes for dinner. Have you been with your friends this afternoon?"

Alicia grabbed Mom around the waist and held on tight. "I missed you so much. Micah and I—"

"Well, this hug is really nice. I love you too," said her mother, hugging back. "But I'm trying to get dinner ready. You could have stayed at your friends' a little longer. Dinner won't be done for a few minutes."

"What?" asked Alicia.

Micah gave her a warning glance, shaking his head no. "Hi, Mom," he said and grabbed a cookie from the jar.

"No snacks before dinner," said his mother.

Micah shrugged and put it back. It felt like so long since he'd had a cookie. He waved Alicia toward his father's den. "Let's put the phone back. Maybe Dad'll never notice."

"Fat chance," said Alicia. "It's all banged up."

"I know," said Micah. "The back won't even stay

on. But I'll cover it with a few papers. Maybe he won't notice." He stopped and turned to look at Alicia. "That's the old me talking. The new me says 'I'm going to tell Dad what happened and share my texting journal.'"

"I want Mom and Dad to know everything," said Alicia. "The texting journal is a good idea. I'm going to pull it off my phone right now."

"I'm home," called Dad. He poked his head around the doorway into the den. "Have you kids seen that experimental phone? It malfunctioned a few times, and I was going to dismantle it today, but I forgot to take it to work."

Alicia looked at Micah and giggled.

"We'd love to tell you," said Micah. "But it's a long story, and we have to get ready."

"Ready for what?" asked Dad. "I don't understand."

"Read this while you wait," said Alicia, writing on a scrap of paper from Dad's desk.

"<3 2 B HME!"

Dad smiled. "I love to be home too."

"BRB," said Micah and Alicia together as they raced for their phones to download their texting journals.

ALICIA'S JOURNAL

BRGHMS BDAY PRTY, NO BALLOONS, 1 PRESENT.

THX 4 FOOD, BDAY PRTYS, MOM, WTR PUMP. HLP ME NOT FEEL SRY 4 SELF.

BRGHMS MOM DIED. WRKD HARD. ATE A BIRD.

XOXO MOM, ARMS TIRD, HNGRY, THX 4 BIRDS, HRD DAY—

NO SRY 4 SELF.

MET EMMA SMITH & PROPHET JOSEPH. EMMA = BEAUTIFUL.

HLP ME NOT FEEL SRY 4 SELF AGAIN. TSTMNY—

THX 4 JS, BY, B OF M, TMPLS, AND THE SAVIOR.

BRIGHAM SAVED ME FROM THE RIVER. WAS SCRD.

<3 WRK, NO SRY 4 SELF. I <3 BRGHAM, MISS U HOME.

INDIAN WNTD ME TO GO TO HVN WITH SICK BABY.

SCRD, SCRD, SCRD. THX 4 LIFE! NO NEKLACE, NO SRY 4 SELF.

BRGHMS KIDS HAVE FUN HOME. WANT 2 B HOME, SRY 4 SELF!

LANDED IN THE GRT SLT LK, PRYD 2 GT HME

<3 2 B HOME, MISS U MOM & DAD, ALWS PRY IN MY <3.

ST. GEORGE TMPL LOOKS LIKE A CASTLE FROM HVN.

BRGHM CAN'T WALK.

THX 4 WRK ON TMPL, THX 4 PRYR, PRY, PRY, PRY, <3 HME.

BRGHM LOVES THE TMPL, I LOVE IT TOO. I CAN MAKE RUGS!

THX FOR BRGHM, NO SRY 4 SELF, <3 U MOM & DAD, TSTIMNY.

MICAH'S JOURNAL

BRGHMS BDAY PRTY, BONY FISH, MOLASSES CAKE.

HATE 2 WRK HARD. <3 U MOM, THX 4 HME. GUILT 4 BEING HERE.

GATHERD MAPL SAP, ATE ROBIN SOUP. WRKD HARD, MISS HME.

HNGRY, HNGRY, HNGRY.

MET JOSEPH SMITH, KNOW HE IS A PROPHET.

THX 4 JS, THX 4 B OF M—READ EVRY DAY. THX FOR TMPLS.

BRGHM BUILT A STRNG RAFT TO CROSS RIVER.

GOD WANTS US 2 WRK HRD.

BEGN 2 LIKE WRK, FEEL GOOD INSID, THX 4 LOGS & HORSES.

INDIANS WNTD TO KILL ALICIA. BRGHM BLSSD BABY. IT GOT WELL.

NEVER TAKE FONE AGAIN, GUILT, THX ALICIA SAFE, WNT 2 GO HME.

LRND 2 FENCE, SWAM IN A FONT. MAY B STUCK 4 EVER, GUILT.

I'M SRY ALICIA, WE NEED HLP.

BRGHM HAS A BOAT PWRD BY HORSE. SAW SL TEMPLE NT FNSHD.

PRY, PRY, PRY. THX HVNLY FTHR ANSR 2 PRYR—FONE WRKD.

SEE THE ST. GEORGE TMPL, BPTSML FONT LIKE OLD TSTAMNT ONE.

PRAY TO GET HME. TSTIMNY, WRK ON TMPL.

ST. GEORGE TMPL DONE. HLPD PLNT FLWRS & TREES.

THX 4 TSTIMNY, THX FOR BRGHM, THX FOR TMPLS, THX 4 HRD WRK.

ENDNOTES

Chapter 2

1. S. Dilworth Young, *Here Is Brigham* (Salt Lake City: Bookcraft, 1964), 32.
2. Leonard J. Arrington, "Brigham Young," in *The Presidents of the Church* (Salt Lake City: Deseret Book, 1986), 44.
3. Young, *Here Is Brigham*, 25.

Chapter 3

1. Lynda Cory Robison, *Boys Who Became Prophets* (Salt Lake City: Deseret Book, 1982), 12.

Chapter 4

1. Richard F Palmer and Karl D. Butler, *The New York Years Brigham Young* (Provo, Utah: Charles Redd Center for Western Studies, Brigham Young University, 1982), 6–7.

Chapter 5

1. Leonard J. Arrington, *Brigham Young, American Moses* (New York: Alfred A. Knopf, 1985), 34.
2. Preston Nibley, *Brigham Young: The Man and His Work* (Salt Lake City: Deseret Book, 1970), 11.
3. Joseph Smith Papers, KBYU Documentary, aired Aug. 15, 2010.

4. Brigham Young, *Discourses of Brigham Young*, sel. John A. Widtsoe (Salt Lake City: Deseret Book), 411, as cited in *Teachings of the Presidents of the Church: Brigham Young* (Salt Lake City: Church of Jesus Christ of Latter-day Saints, 1997), 300.

Chapter 6

1. Arrington, *Brigham Young, American Moses*, 130.
2. Young, *Discourses of Brigham Young*, sel. John A. Widtsoe, as cited in *Teachings of the Presidents of the Church: Brigham Young*, 228.
3. Arrington, *Brigham Young, American Moses*, 139–40.

Chapter 7

1. Dean C. Jessee, ed., *Letters of Brigham Young to His Sons*, (Salt Lake City: Deseret Book, 1974), 263–64.
2. Clarissa Young Spencer with Mabel Harmer, *Brigham Young at Home* (Salt Lake City: Deseret Book, 1974), 113.
3. Ibid., 126–27.
4. Ibid., 133–34.

Chapter 8

1. Arrington, *Brigham Young, American Moses*, 210.
2. Spencer with Harmer, *Brigham Young at Home*, 30–31.
3. Ibid., 34.
4. Ibid., 31.
5. Ibid.
6. Ibid., 34.
7. Ibid., 150.
8. Ibid., 151.

Chapter 9

1. Spencer with Harmer, *Brigham Young at Home*, 177–78.
2. Ibid., 178.
3. Susan Evans McCloud, *Brigham Young, An Inspiring Personal Biography* (American Fork, UT: Covenant Communications, 1996), 267.
4. Ibid.

5. Young, *Discourses of Brigham Young*, 395.
6. Spencer with Harmer, *Brigham Young at Home*, 32.
7. D&C 9:7–8
8. Young, *Discourses of Brigham Young*, 456, as cited in *Teachings of the Presidents of the Church: Brigham Young*, 343.

Chapter 10

1. "St. George Temple: One Hundred Years of Service."
2. Ibid.
3. Ibid.
4. Nibley, *Brigham Young: The Man and His Work*, 475.
5. "St. George Temple: One Hundred Years of Service," *Ensign*, March 1977.
6. Enos 1; D&C 9:7–8

Chapter 11

1. Susa Young Gates, *The Life Story of Brigham Young* (London: Jarrolds Publishers, 1930), 180.
2. "St. George Temple: One Hundred Years of Service."
3. Brigham Young, *Deseret News Semi-Weekly*, 16 Jan. 1877, 1, as cited in *Teachings of the Presidents of the Church: Brigham Young*, 299.
4. Brigham Young, *Journal of Discourses* (Salt Lake City: Deseret Book) 18:303–5, as cited in "St. George Temple: One Hundred Years of Service."
5. John Nuttall's Journal, 1 Jan. 1877, as cited in "St. George Temple: One Hundred Years of Service."
6. Ibid.
7. Nibley, *Brigham Young: The Man and His Work*, 100.
8. Brigham Young, *Deseret News Weekly*, 24 Aug. 1854, as cited in *Teachings of the Presidents of the Church: Brigham Young*, viii.
9. Matthew 16:19

DISCUSSION QUESTIONS

1. Micah thought he could fix his dad's phone. Could he? Was it right for him to just take it without asking? What would you do if you were in his place?

2. Were Micah and Alicia honest when they told Brigham where they came from? How did they explain the electronic age? Would you have done it differently?

3. How did Brigham's actions show he loved his mother? How do you show your mother you love her?

4. Micah felt guilty for not helping with the work. What could he have done differently? Have you ever felt guilty for not helping? Give an example.

5. Begin your own texting journal. What are your goals? What are you thankful for?

6. How did Micah and Alicia feel the first time they met Joseph Smith? How do you think you would feel if you met Joseph Smith?

7. How did Brigham answer the question, "Why doesn't God make it easier for you to get across the river?" Does God do our work for us? Why or why not?

8. What did Brigham do when Don Carlos skipped school? What did Don Carlos learn from driving the teams? What did he finally decide about school?

9. How did Micah feel when he was on the Salt Lake Temple grounds? How do you feel when you're on the temple grounds?

10. When Micah and Alicia went to Brigham's family prayer, what did they learn? What had they forgotten to do?

11. When Micah wondered why Heavenly Father wasn't answering his prayers, what did Brigham tell him?

12. Micah said Heavenly Father would bless them if they did His work. Can you think of a time Heavenly Father has blessed you when you've done his work?

ABOUT THE AUTHOR

CHRISTY Monson has always loved pioneer history, especially stories of the prophets. She received her BA degree from Utah State University and an MS from University of Nevada at Las Vegas. After her six children were raised, she established a successful marriage and family therapy practice. She has published articles in the *Ensign, Friend,* and other children's periodicals. She and her husband, Robert, live in Ogden, Utah.